THE OTHER & SONG BOOK

Compiled by Dave Anderson

The Fellowship Publications
Phoenix, AZ 85076

ISBN 0-9628303-2-1 (Spiral Bound)

ISBN 0-9628303-3-X (Perfect Bound)

The Other Songbook, © 1984, 1987 by Dave Anderson.
The Fellowship Publications, P.O. Box 51510, Phoenix, AZ 85076

Printed in the United States of America.

Welcome to THE OTHER SONGBOOK—to songs of praise and truth about God's love and faithfulness.

You will find classic hymns of faith, old gospel favorites, children's songs (some of which you probably haven't sung for years), and many new songs of praise and worship...all right here!

Every Christian knows that the expression of praise through music and singing is special to God. The musician is one of the first occupations mentioned in Scripture (Genesis 4:21). Did you know God created us with a greater capacity to feel and think and remember when music is involved? It's true. And my prayer is that Christians all over the world will use more music to remember God's promises.

"Rev. Dick Hamlin has said:

"Music prepares the heart for worship and commitment. Music is the greatest mood alternator of all, and unlocks the ministry of God in the untrespassed soil of a person's soul. People love singing. They love being moved even when there is not a song in their hearts."

You will enjoy this book. Begin by singing through the books of the Old and New Testaments—memorize both songs and you can start humming when someone tells you to turn to Ezekiel.

Sing your way along a 500-year-old path of wonderful, simple, profound Christian songs. Let God touch your soul and mind, ministering His joy and comfort to you as you sing one song after another.

Truth must be sung!

Why the unique name? Your church already has an "official" book of songs. This is THE OTHER SONGBOOK!

Dave Anderson

HOW MAJESTIC IS YOUR NAME 1

Michael W. Smith
Arr. by Henry Wiens

2   A MIGHTY FORTRESS

Martin Luther
Tr., Frederick Henry Hedge

Martin Luther
Arr., Traditional

3 ALL DAY SONG

Words and Music by
John Fischer

1. Love Him in the morn - in' when you see the sun a - ris in',
2. And in the in be-tween time when you feel the pres - sure com - in',

Love Him in the eve - nin' cause He took you through the day; —
Re-mem-ber that He loves you and He prom - is - es to stay. —

Fine

When you think you got to wor - ry 'cause it

seems the thing to do; Re-mem - ber He ain't in a hur-

ry. He's al- ways got time for you.

D.C. al Fine

ALL HAIL THE POWER

4

Oliver Holden
Arr., Roger Nachtway

1. All hail the pow'r of Je - sus' Name! Let an - gels pros - trate fall; Bring forth the roy - al di - a - dem, And crown him Lord of ___ all. Bring forth the roy - al di - a - dem, And crown him Lord ____ of all.
2. Crown him, ye morn - ing stars of light, Who fixed this earth - ly ball; Now hail the strength of Is - rael's might, And crown him Lord of ___ all. Now hail the strength of Is - rael's __ might, And crown him Lord ____ of all.
3. Sin - ners whose love can ne'er for - get The worm-wood and the gall, Go spread your tro - phies at __ his __ feet, And crown him Lord of ___ all. Go spread your tro - phies at __ his __ feet, And crown him Lord ____ of all.
4. Let ev - 'ry kin - dred, ev - 'ry tribe On this ter - res - trial ball To him all maj - es - ty __ as - cribe, And crown him Lord of ___ all. To him all maj - es - ty __ as - cribe, And crown him Lord ____ of all.
5. O that with yon - der sa - cred throng We at his feet may fall; We'll join the ev - er - last - ing __ song, And crown him Lord of ___ all. We'll join the ev - er - last - ing __ song, And crown him Lord ____ of all.

5

ALL THY WORKS
SHALL PRAISE THEE

Ps. 145: 10-13
Adapted by D. G.

Dale Garratt

ALLELUIA

6

Jerry Sinclair
Dino Prod.

With quiet adoration

1. Al - le - lu - ia, ____ Al - le - lu - ia, ____ Al - le -
lu - ia, ____ Al - le - lu - ia, ____ Al - le - lu - ia. ____

2. How I love him   3. Blessed Jesus   4. My Redeemer   5. Jesus is Lord   6. Alleluia

7 BE STILL, MY SOUL

Katharina von Schlegel
Tr. by Jane L. Borthwick

Jean Sibelius

1. Be still, my soul: the Lord is on thy side; _____ Bear pa - tient - ly the cross of grief or pain; _____ Leave to thy God to or - der and pro - vide; _____ In ev - ery change He faith - ful will re - main. _____ Be still, my soul: thy

2. Be still, my soul: thy God doth un - der - take _____ To guide the fu - ture as He has the past. _____ Thy hope, thy con - fi - dence let noth - ing shake; _____ All now mys - te - rious shall be bright at last. _____ Be still, my soul: the

3. Be still, my soul: the hour is has - tening on _____ When we shall be for - ev - er with the Lord, _____ When dis - ap - point - ment, grief, and fear are gone, _____ Sor - row for - got, love's pur - est joys re - stored. _____ Be still, my soul: when

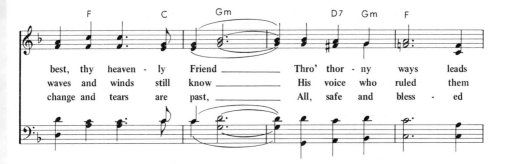

best, thy heaven - ly Friend _____ Thro' thor - ny ways leads
waves and winds still know _____ His voice who ruled them
change and tears are past, _____ All, safe and bless - ed

to a joy - ful end _____
while He dwelt be - low. _____
we shall meet at last. _____ A - men.

LORD, LAY SOME SOUL UPON MY HEART   8

Dr. Leon Tucker

David H. Johnson

Lord, lay some soul up - on my heart, And love that soul thru me; ___

And may I hum - bly do my part To win that soul for Thee. ___

9 BEAUTIFUL SAVIOR

Munster Gesangbuch
Tr. Joseph A. Seiss

Silesian Folk-Tune
Hoffmann von Fallersleben's Volkslieder

1. Beau - ti - ful Sav - ior! King of cre - a - tion!
2. Fair are the mead - ows, Fair - er the wood - lands,
3. Fair is the sun - shine, Fair - er the moon - light
4. Beau - ti - ful Sav - ior! Lord of the na - tions!

Son of God and Son of Man!
Robed in flow'rs of bloom - ing spring;
And the spark - ling stars on high;
Son of God and Son of Man!

Tru - ly I'd love Thee, Tru - ly I'd serve Thee,
Je - sus is fair - er; Je - sus is pur - er;
Je - sus shines bright - er, Je - sus shines pur - er;
Glo - ry and hon - or, Praise, a - dor - a - tion,

Light of my soul, my joy, my crown!
He makes our sorrow - ing spir it sing.
Than all the an - gels in the sky.
Now and for - ev - er - more be Thine!

BEHOLD WHAT MANNER OF LOVE

10

Words and Music by
Patricia Van Tine

Be - hold what man - ner of love the Fa - ther has giv - en un - to us! Be - hold what man - ner of love the Fa - ther has giv - en un - to us! That we should be called the chil - dren of God, That we should be called the chil - dren of God.

11 BECAUSE HE LIVES

W. J. and Gloria Gaither

William J. Gaither

1. God sent His Son, they called Him Je - sus;
2. How sweet to hold a new - born ba - by
3. And then one day I'll cross the riv - er;

He came to love, heal, and for - give.
And feel the pride and joy He gives;
I'll fight life's fi nal war with pain.

He lived and died to buy my par - don;
But great - er still the calm as - sur - ance
And then as death gives way to vic - tory,

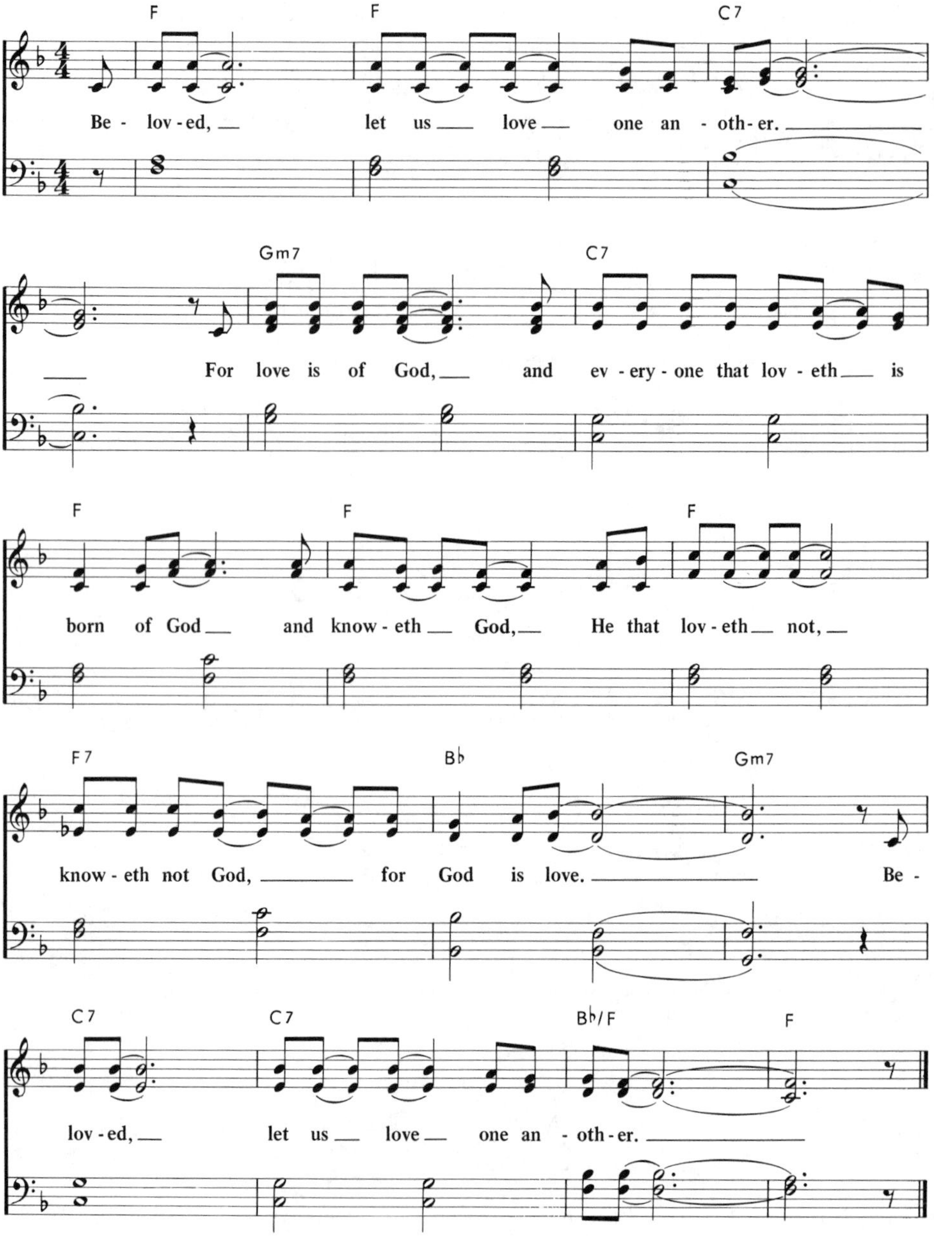

BELOVED, LET US LOVE ONE ANOTHER

I John 4: 7,8

Dennis Ryder

F F C7
Be - lov - ed, let us love one an - oth - er.
Gm7 C7
For love is of God, and ev - ery - one that lov - eth is
F F F
born of God and know - eth God, He that lov - eth not,
F7 B♭ Gm7
know - eth not God, for God is love. Be -
C7 C7 B♭/F F
lov - ed, let us love one an - oth - er.

BLESS HIS HOLY NAME

13

Ps. 103: 1-2

Andraé Crouch

Bless the Lord, O my soul, _____ and all that is with-in me, Bless His ho - ly _____ Name.

Fine

He has done great things, _____ He has done great things, _____

He has done great things, Bless His ho - ly Name.

D.C. al Fine

BIND US TOGETHER

Bob Gillman

LORD, BE GLORIFIED

15

Words and Music by
Bob Kilpatrick

D.C. al Fine

1. In my life Lord, Be glo - ri - fied, be glo - ri - fied.
2. In my song Lord, Be glo - ri - fied, be glo - ri - fied.
3. In Your church Lord, Be glo - ri - fied, be glo - ri - fied.

In my life Lord, Be glo - ri - fied to - day.
In my song Lord, Be glo - ri - fied to - day.
In Your church Lord, Be glo - ri - fied to - day.

16 BLESSED ASSURANCE

Fanny J. Crosby

Mrs. J. F. Knapp

1. Bless - ed as - sur - ance, Je - sus is mine! __ Oh, what a fore - taste of glo - ry di - vine! __ Heir of sal - va - tion, pur - chase of God, __ Born of His Spir - it, washed in His blood. __
2. Per - fect sub - mis - sion, per - fect de - light, __ Vi - sions of rap - ture now burst on my sight; __ An - gels de - scend - ing, bring from a - bove __ Ech - oes of mer - cy, whis - pers of love. __
3. Per - fect sub - mis - sion, all is at rest, __ I in my Sav - ior am hap - py and blest; __ Watch-ing and wait - ing, look - ing a - bove, __ Filled with His good - ness, lost in His love. __

Chorus

This is my sto - ry, this is my song, __ Prais-ing my Sav - ior all the day long; __ This is my sto - ry,

This is my song,___ Prais-ing my Sav - ior all the day long. ___

HEAVENLY SUNSHINE 17

Arr. by Charles E. Fuller

Heav - en - ly sun - shine, heav - en - ly sun - shine, Flood-ing my

soul with glo - ry di - vine,___ Heav - en - ly sun - shine, heav - en - ly

sun - shine, Hal - le - lu - jah! Je - sus is mine! ___

18 BOOKS OF THE OLD TESTAMENT

Words Arr. by
Mrs. W. I. M. Tabor

Tune: "Did You Ever See A Lassie"
Arr. by Gordon E. Hooker

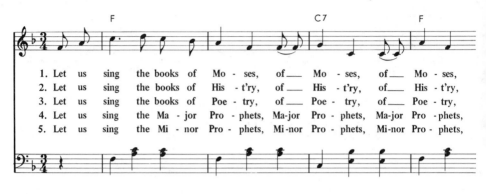

1. Let us sing the books of Mo - ses, of __ Mo - ses, of __ Mo - ses,
2. Let us sing the books of His - t'ry, of __ His - t'ry, of __ His - t'ry,
3. Let us sing the books of Poe - try, of __ Poe - try, of __ Poe - try,
4. Let us sing the Ma - jor Pro - phets, Ma-jor Pro - phets, Major Pro - phets,
5. Let us sing the Mi - nor Pro - phets, Mi-nor Pro - phets, Mi-nor Pro - phets,

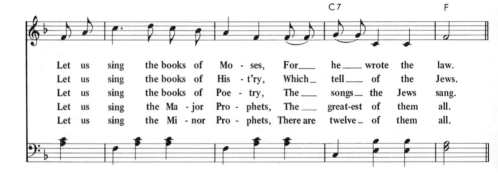

Let us sing the books of Mo - ses, For __ he __ wrote the law.
Let us sing the books of His - t'ry, Which __ tell __ of the Jews.
Let us sing the books of Poe - try, The __ songs __ the Jews sang.
Let us sing the Ma - jor Pro - phets, The __ great-est of them all.
Let us sing the Mi - nor Pro - phets, There are twelve __ of them all.

(2nd Verse only)

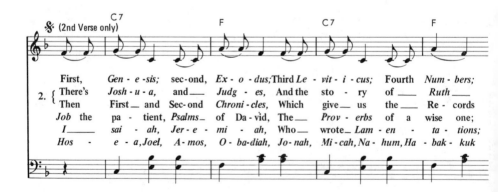

     First,   Gen - e -sis; sec-ond, Ex - o - dus;Third Le - vit - i - cus; Fourth Num - bers;
2. { There's Josh - u - a, and __ Judg - es, And the sto - ry of __ Ruth __
    Then   First __ and Sec- ond Chroni - cles, Which give __ us the __ Re - cords
Job the pa - tient, Psalms __ of Da - vid, The __ Prov - erbs of a wise one;
I __ sai - ah, Jer - e - mi - ah, Who __ wrote __ Lam - en - ta - tions;
Hos - e - a,Joel, A - mos, O - ba-diah, Jo - nah, Mi - cah,Na - hum,Ha - bak - kuk

C7   F

And the fifth   is *Deu-ter - on - o - my,* The— last of them — all

2. { Then — *First* *and Sec-ond Sam-u - el,* And— *First* *and* *Sec -ond Kings.*

Then — *Ez - ra, Ne- he - mi - ah,* And— *Es - ther,* the — Queen.

And — then   *Ec -cles - i - as - tes,* And the *Song* *of* *Sol - o - mon.*

Then *E - ze - kiel* and — *Dan - iel,* Who were true to their — God.

Zeph -a - ni - ah, Hag - ga - i, *Zech- a - ri - ah,* *Mal - a - chi.*

D.S. (2nd Verse only)

JESUS LOVES
THE LITTLE CHILDREN

19

George F. Root

Je - sus loves the lit - tle chil - dren, — All the chil - dren of the

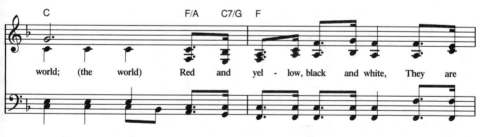

world; (the world) Red and yel - low, black and white, They are

pre - cious in His sight; Je - sus loves the lit - tle chil - dren of the world.

20 BREAK FORTH INTO JOY

Unknown

CLEANSE ME

J. Edwin Orr.

Maori Melody, Arranged

1. Search me, O God, and know my heart to-day;
   Try me, O Savior, know my thoughts, I pray:
   See if there be some wick-ed way in me:
   Cleanse me from ev-'ry sin and set me free.

2. I praise Thee, Lord, for cleans-ing me from sin:
   Ful-fill Thy Word, and make me pure with-in;
   Fill me with fire, where once I burned with shame:
   Grant my de-sire to mag-ni-fy Thy name.

3. Lord, take my life, and make it whol-ly Thine;
   Fill my poor heart with Thy great love di-vine;
   Take all my will, my pas-sion, self and pride;
   I now sur-ren-der: Lord, in me a-bide.

4. O Ho-ly Ghost, re-viv-al comes from Thee:
   Send a re-viv-al start the work in me:
   Thy Word de-clares Thou wilt sup-ply our need:
   For bless-ing now, O Lord, I hum-bly plead.

22 BRIGHTEN THE CORNER
WHERE YOU ARE

Ina Duley Ogdon

Charles H. Gabriel

1. Do not wait un - til some deed of great - ness you may do, Do not
2. Just a - bove are cloud - ed skies that you may help to clear, Let not
3. Here for all your tal - ent you may sure - ly find a need, Here re -

wait to shed your light a - far; To the man - y du -ties ev - er near you
nar - row self your way de - bar; Tho in - to one heart a - lone may fall your
flect the Bright and Morn-ing Star; E - ven from your hum-ble hand the bread of

now be true, Bright - en the cor-ner where you are.
song of cheer, Bright - en the cor-ner where you are. Bright - en the cor-ner
life may feed, Bright - en the cor-ner where you are.

where you are! Bright - en the cor - ner where you are! Some-one far from

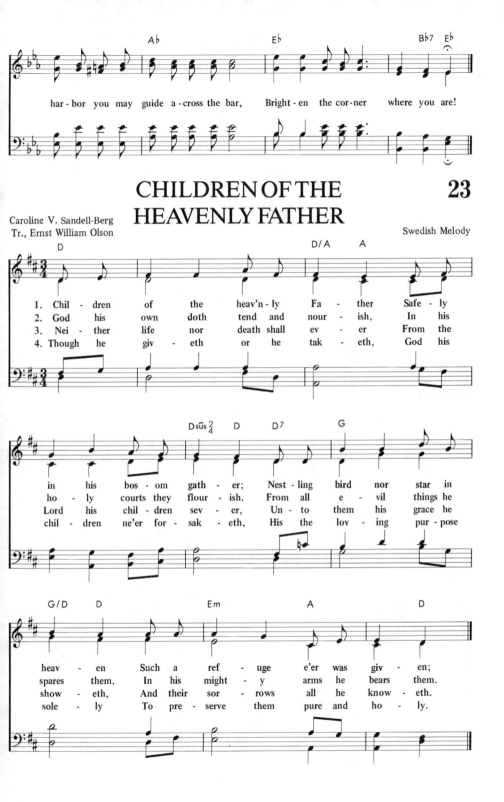

har - bor you may guide a - cross the bar, Bright - en the cor - ner where you are!

CHILDREN OF THE HEAVENLY FATHER

23

Caroline V. Sandell-Berg
Tr., Ernst William Olson

Swedish Melody

1. Chil - dren of the heav'n - ly Fa - ther Safe - ly
2. God his own doth tend and nour - ish, In his
3. Nei - ther life nor death shall ev - er From the
4. Though he giv - eth or he tak - eth, God his

in his bos - om gath - er; Nest - ling bird nor star in
ho - ly courts they flour - ish. From all e - vil things he
Lord his chil - dren sev - er, Un - to them his grace he
chil - dren ne'er for - sak - eth, His the lov - ing pur - pose

heav - en Such a ref - uge e'er was giv - en;
spares them, In his might - y arms he bears them.
show - eth, And their sor - rows all he know - eth.
sole - ly To pre - serve them pure and ho - ly.

24 THE BUTTERFLY SONG

Words and Music by
Brian Howard

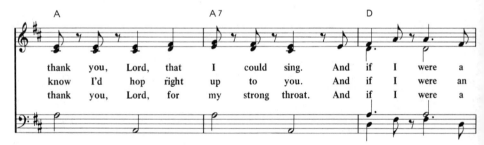

25 CALVARY COVERS IT ALL

Mrs. Walter G. Tayler

1. Far dear-er than all that the world can im-part Was the mes-sage that
2. The stripes that He bore and the thorns that He wore Told His mer-cy and
3. How match-less the grace, when I looked in the face ___ Of Je-sus, my
4. How bless-ed the tho't that my soul by Him bought ___ Shall dwell in the

came to my heart (to my heart), ___ How Je-sus a-lone for my
love ev-er-more (ev-er-more); ___ My heart bowed in shame as I
cru-ci-fied Lord (of my Lord); My re-demp-tion com-plete, I then
glo-ry on high (dwell on high), Where with glad-ness and song I'll be

sin did a-tone, And Cal-va-ry cov-ers it all. ___
called on His name, And Cal-va-ry cov-ers it all. ___
found at His feet, And Cal-va-ry cov-ers it all. ___
one of the throng And Cal-va-ry cov-ers it all. ___

cov-ers it all.

Chorus

Cal-va-ry cov-ers it all. My past with its sin and stain: My

guilt and de-spair Je-sus took on Him there, And Cal - va-ry cov-ers it all.

HAVE THINE OWN WAY   26

Adelaide A. Pollard

G. C. Stebbins

1. Have thine own way, Lord, have thine own way! ___ Thou art the Pot - ter; I am the clay. __ Mould me and make me Af - ter thy will, ___ While I am wait - ing, Yield - ed and still. ___

2. Have thine own way, Lord, have thine own way! ___ Search me and try me, Mas - ter, to day! __ Whit - er than snow, Lord, Wash me just now, ___ As in thy pres - ence Hum - bly I bow. ___

3. Have thine own way, Lord, have thine own way! ___ Wound- ed and wea - ry, Help me, I pray! __ Pow - er, all pow - er, Sure - ly is thine! ___ Touch me and heal me, Sav - ior di - vine! ___

4. Have thine own way, Lord, have thine own way! ___ Hold o'er my be - ing, Ab - so lute sway! __ Fill with thy Spir - it, Till all shall see ___ Christ on - ly, al - ways, Liv - ing in me! ___

27 CHARITY

Adapted from I Cor. 13.

Words and Music by
Kenn Gulliksen
Arr. by Henry Wiens

1. Al - though I speak with tongues of men and
2. Love is patient and kind. Love is not
3. One sea - son I was a child I spoke and I

an - gels, and though I pro - phe - sy
en - vi - ous not proud, but gen - tle and meek
thought as a child But when I turn - ed to man

and un - der - stand all. Al - though I
seeks not its own way. Love sings when
such ways put a - side. Tho' now we

have all faith so moun - tains may be re - moved
Je - sus pre - vails Be - lieves and en - dures all things
see thru a glass yet then we shall see face to face

And though I feed the poor and give up my
Love hopes and bears every wrong and Love nev - er
Though now a - bide faith and hope the great - est is

life _____
fails _____
love _____
If I have not char - i - ty

If love does not flow from me I am

noth - ing Jesus re - duce me to love _____

1. 2.

3.

love _____ Jesus re - duce me to love. _____

Fine

28 COME AND PRAISE THE LORD

Ps. 118:1-7, 22-23
Steffi Geiser Rubin

Stuart Dauermann

1. Give___ thanks___ to the Lord___ for His good-ness;_____ His
2. In my trou - ble I asked___ Him to save me. _____ He
3. The___ Lord,___ my Re - deem - er, is for me;_____ No
4. The___ stone___ which the build - ers re - ject-ed _____ The

faith - ful love en - dur - eth for - ev - er._____
an - swered ___ and set ___ me in safe - ty. _____
more _____ can the wick - ed de - stroy me._____
Lord has made the cor - ner-stone for all. _____

Come and praise the Lord, come and praise the Lord, For His mer-cy is

1. won-drous in our eyes._____

2. won-drous in our eyes._____

COME BLESS THE LORD

Dale and Evelyn
Hunter

Ps. 134: 1,2

30 COME ON, RING THOSE BELLS

Words and Music by
Andrew Culverwell

1. Ev-'ry-bod-y likes to take a hol-i-day, __ Ev-'ry-bod-y likes to take a rest
2. Cel-e-bra-tions come be-cause of some-thing good, __ cele-bra-tions we love to re-call.

spend-ing time to-geth-er with the fam-i-ly, __
Mar-y had a ba-by boy in Beth-le-hem, __ the

shar-ing lots of love __ and hap-pi-ness. ____
great-est cel-e-bra-tion of them all. ____

Come on, ring those bells,

light the Christ-mas tree. __ Je-sus is the King __ born for you and me. __

Come on, ring those bells, ev-'ry-bod-y say, "Je-sus, we re-mem-ber this your birth - day."

AMAZING GRACE

31

John Newton

1. A - maz - ing grace! how sweet the sound, That
2. 'Twas grace that taught my heart to fear, And
3. Thro' man - y dan - gers, toils and snares, I
4. When we've been there ten thou – sand years, Bright

saved a wretch like me! I once____ was lost, but
grace my fears re - lieved, How pre - cious did that
have al - read - y come; 'Tis grace____ hath bro't me
shin - ing as the sun, We've no____ less days to

now____ am found, Was blind, but now I see.
grace____ ap - pear The hour I first be - lieved!
safe____ thus far, And grace will lead me home.
sing ____ God's praise Than when we first be - gun.

32 COME, THOU ALMIGHTY KING

Anonymous

Felice Glardini

1. Come, Thou al - might - y King, Help us Thy name to sing,
2. Je - sus, our Lord, de - scend; From all our foes de - fend,
3. Come, Thou in - car - nate Word, Gird on Thy might - y sword,

Help us to praise! Fa - ther all glo - ri - ous, O'er all vic -
Nor let us fall; Let Thine al - might - y aid Our sure de -
Our pray'r at - tend. Come and Thy peo - ple bless, And give Thy

to - ri - ous, Come and reign o - ver us, An - cient of Days!
fense be made: Our souls on Thee be stay'd; Lord, hear our call!
word suc - cess; Spir - it of ho - li - ness, On us de - scend.

4. Come, holy Comforter,
Thy sacred witness bear
In this glad hour;
Thou who almighty art,
Now rule in every heart,
And ne'er from us depart,
Spirit of power!

5. To the great One in Three
Eternal praises be,
Hence evermore;
His sovereign majesty
May we in glory see,
And to eternity
Love and adore.

COME, THOU FOUNT OF EVERY BLESSING

Robert Robinson

Asahel Nettleton

1. Come, Thou Fount of ev-'ry bless-ing, Tune my heart to sing Thy grace;
2. Here I raise my Eb-en-e-zer, Hith-er by Thy help I'm come;
3. O to grace how great a debt-or, Dai-ly I'm con-strained to be;

Streams of mer-cy, nev-er ceas-ing, Call for songs of loud-est praise.
And I hope, by Thy good pleas-ure, Safe-ly to ar-rive at home.
Let that grace now like a fet-ter, Bind my wan-d'ring heart to Thee.

While the hope of end-less glo-ry Fills my heart with joy and love,
Je-sus sought me when a stran-ger, Wand'ring from the fold of God;
Prone to wan-der, Lord, I feel it, Prone to leave the God I love;

Teach me ev-er to a-dore Thee, May I still Thy good-ness prove.
He, to res-cue me from dan-ger, In-ter-posed His pre-cious blood.
Here's my heart, O take and seal it, Seal it for Thy courts a-bove.

34 COMMUNION SONG

Words and Music by
Barry McGuire

1. Take this bread I give to you, And as you do, re - mem - ber me. This bread is my bod -y bro-ken just for you. Take it, (take it), eat it: (eat it): Each time you do, re - mem - ber me, re - mem - ber me.

2. Take this cup I fill for you, And as you do, re - mem - ber me. This cup is the new cove-nant I'm mak - ing with you. Take it, (take it), drink it: (drink it): Each time you do, re - mem - ber me, re - mem - ber me.

3. Take this love I've giv - en you, And as you do, re - mem - ber

Coda: me, re - mem - ber me, re - mem - ber me;

COME TO MY HEART, LORD JESUS

35

Emily E. S. Elliott

Timothy Richard Matthews

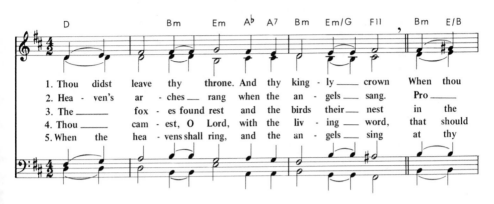

1. Thou didst leave thy throne. And thy king - ly ___ crown When thou
2. Hea - ven's ar - ches ___ rang when the an - gels ___ sang. Pro ___
3. The ___ fox - es found rest and the birds their ___ nest in the
4. Thou ___ cam - est, O Lord, with the liv - ing ___ word, that should
5. When the hea - vens shall ring, and the an - gels ___ sing at thy

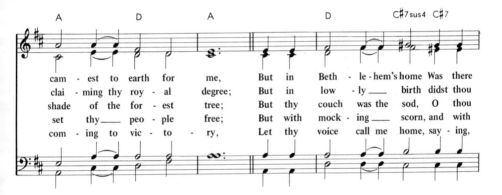

cam - est to earth for me, But in Beth - le - hem's home Was there
clai - ming thy roy - al degree; But in low - ly ___ birth didst thou
shade of the for - est tree; But thy couch was the sod, O thou
set thy ___ peo - ple free; But with mock - ing ___ scorn, and with
com - ing to vic - to - ry, Let thy voice call me home, say - ing,

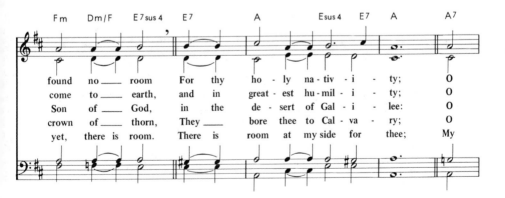

found no ___ room For thy ho - ly na - tiv - i - ty; O
come to ___ earth, and in great - est hu - mil - i - ty; O
Son of ___ God, in the de - sert of Gal - i - lee: O
crown of ___ thorn, They ___ bore thee to Cal - va - ry; O
yet, there is room. There is room at my side for thee; My

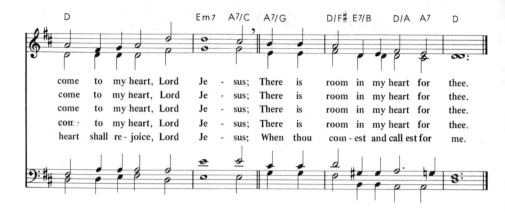

36 FINALLY HOME

L. E. Singer and Don Wyrtzen

Don Wyrtzen
Arr. by Henry Wiens

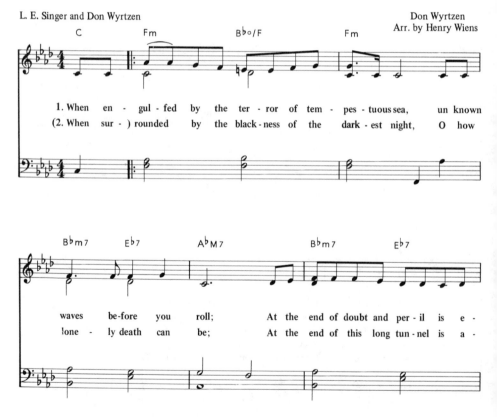

37 HOW EXCELLENT IS THY NAME

Words and Music by
Dick Tunney, Melody Tunney
and Paul Smith
Arr. by Henry Wiens

39 DAY BY DAY

Words and Music by
Caroline V. Sandell-Berg

1. Day by day and with each pass-ing mo-ment, Strength I find to
2. Ev-'ry day the Lord him-self is near me, With a spe-cial
3. Help me then, in ev-'ry trib-u-la-tion, So to trust Thy

meet my tri-als here. Trust-ing in my Fa-ther's wise be-stow-ment,
mer-cy for each hour. All my cares He fain would bear and cheer me,
prom-is-es, O Lord, That I lose not faith's sweet con-so-la-tion,

I've no cause for wor-ry or for fear. He whose heart is kind be-yond all
He whose name is Coun-sel-or and Pow'r The pro-tec-tion of His child and
Of-fered me with-in Thy ho-ly Word. Help me, Lord, when toil and trou-ble

meas-ure Gives un-to each day what He deems best, Lov-ing-ly its
treas-ure Is a charge that on him-self He laid. "As thy days, thy
meet-ing, E'er to take, as from a Fa-ther's hand, One by one the

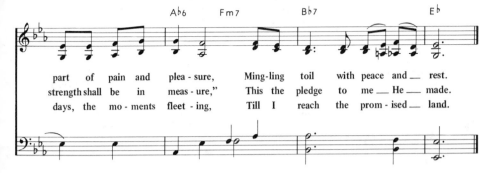

part of pain and plea - sure, Ming-ling toil with peace and __ rest.
strength shall be in meas - ure," This the pledge to me __ He __ made.
days, the mo - ments fleet - ing, Till I reach the prom - ised __ land.

FATHER, I ADORE YOU

40

Words and Music by
Terrye Coelho

1. Fa - ther, I a - dore You, Lay my life be -
2. Je - sus
3. Spir - it

fore You. How I love You;

41   DO, LORD! : PSALM 27

Adapted by J. Y. from Ps. 27, Eph. 3:21

Traditional
Arr. by John Ylvisaker

42 EASTER SONG

Words and Music by
Anne Herring

1. Hear the bells ring - ing, they're sing - ing that we can be born a - gain!
2. Hear the bells ring - ing, they're sing - ing, "Christ is ris - en from the dead!"

The an - gel up - on the tomb - stone said, "He is ris - en just as He said,

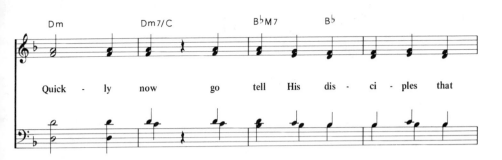

Quick - ly now go tell His dis - ci - ples that

Je - sus Christ is no long - er dead!"

Joy to the world, He is ris - en, Al -

le - lu - ia! He's ris - en, Al - le - lu - ia! He's

ris - en, Al - le - lu - ia!

43

FILL MY CUP, LORD

Words and Music by Richard Blanchard
Arr. by Eugene Clark

1. Like the wom-an at the well I was seek-ing _____ For things that could not sat-is-fy. And then I heard my Sav-ior speak-ing: "Draw from my well that nev-er shall run dry."

2. There are mil-lions in this world who are crav-ing _____ The pleas-ure earth-ly things af-ford. But none can match the won-drous treas-ure _____ That I find in Je-sus Christ, my Lord.

3. So my broth-er, if the things this world gave you _____ Leaves hun-gers that won't pass a-way. My bless-ed Lord will come and save you _____ If you kneel to Him and hum-bly pray.

Chorus

Fill my cup, Lord,— I lift it up, Lord.— Come and quench this thirst-ing of my soul.

Bread of heav-en, feed me till I want no more; Fill my cup, fill it up and make me whole.

FATHER, WE THANK YOU 44

John 15:26; I John 4:9,19

Gary Johnson

1. Fa - ther, we thank You; Fa -
2. Je - sus, we thank You; Je -
3. Fa - ther, we love You; Fa -

ther, we thank You for giv - ing to
sus, we thank You for giv - ing to
ther, we thank You be - cause You have

us Your Son; ___ Fa - ther, we thank You.
us Your Spir - it; Je - sus, we thank You.
first loved us; ___ Fa - ther, we love You.

45 FOR GOD SO LOVED

John 1:10-12, 3:16-17

Words and Music by
Stuart Dauermann

1. For God so loved the world that He gave ____ His ____
2. For God did not send His ____ Son in-to the world ____
3. He came in-to the world and He dwelt a-mong His own; but His

on - ly be - got - ten Son, ___ That who - so - ev - er be ___
____ to ____ bring ___ con-dem - na - tion; But rath - er that through the re -
own they would not ____ re - ceive. ____ But pow'r to be - come the ____

lieves in ___ Him ____ should not per - ish, ___ But
ceiv - ing of Him, ____ men might find ____ sal - va - tion And
sons of ___ God He gave to all ___ who be - lieved. ____ He

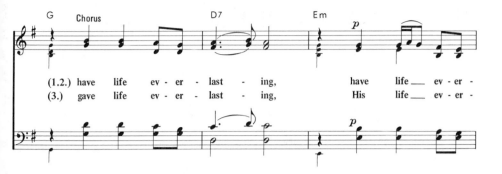

(1.2.) have life ev - er - last - ing, have life ___ ev - er -
(3.) gave life ev - er - last - ing, His life ___ ev - er -

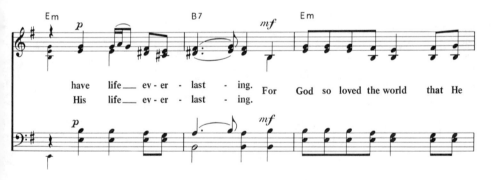

last - ing, have life ev - er - last - ing.
last - ing, His life ev - er - last - ing.

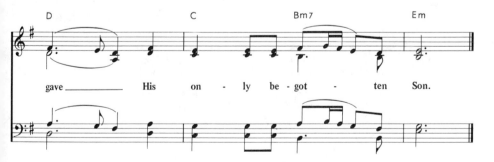

have life ___ ev - er - last - ing. For God so loved the world that He
His life ___ ev - er - last - ing.

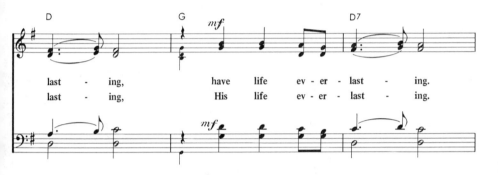

gave _____ His on - ly be - got - ten Son.

46 FOR THOSE TEARS I DIED

Words and Music by
Marsha J. Stevens

1. You said you'd come and share all my sorrows;
2. Your goodness so great I can't understand, And
3. Jesus, I give you my heart and my soul. I

You said you'd be there for all my tomorrows.
dear Lord, I know that all this was planned.
know now without God I'd never be whole.

I came so close to sending you away, But
I know you're here now and always will be. Your
Savior, you opened all the right doors, And I

just as you promised you came there to stay,
love loosed my chains from earth's humble shores,
thank you and praise you and in you I'm free,

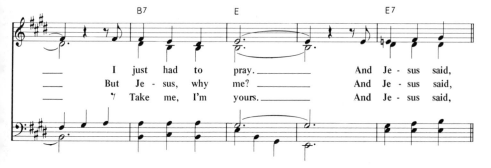

I just had to pray._____ And Je - sus said,
But Je - sus, why me? _____ And Je - sus said,
Take me, I'm yours._____ And Je - sus said,

"Come to the wa - ter, stand by my side. I know you are

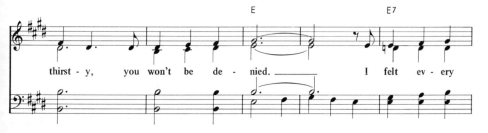

thirst - y, you won't be de - nied. _____ I felt ev - ery

tear - drop when in dark - ness you cried, _____ And I

strove to re - mind you that for those tears I died." _____

47 FREELY, FREELY

Adapted from Matt. 10:7, 8

Words and Music by
Carol Owens

1. God for - gave my sin in Je - sus' name, I've been born a -
2. All____ pow'r is giv'n in Je - sus' name, In____ earth and

gain in Je - sus' name; And in Je - sus' name I come to you To
heav'n in Je - sus' name; And in Je - sus' name I come to you To

share His love as He told me to. He said, "Free - ly, free - ly
share His pow'r as He told me to.

you have re - ceived: Free - ly, free - ly give.____ Go in my

name, and, be - cause you be - lieve, Oth - ers will know that I live."

GENTLE LIKE YOU 48

Words and Music by
Charles F. Brown

1. Je - sus, Je - sus, Ru - ler of might - y men;
2. Je - sus, Je - sus, Friend to the lone - ly soul;
3. Je - sus, Je - sus, Shep - herd of wan - d'ring ones;
4. Je - sus, Je - sus, Sav - ior of trou - bled man;

Je - sus, Je - sus, Make me gen - tle like You.
Je - sus, Je - sus, Love my broth - er thro' me.
Je - sus, Je - sus, Guide me thro' the dark night.
Je - sus, Je - sus, Give me peace in my soul.

49 GLORIFY THY NAME

Words and Music by Donna Adkins
Arranged by Edward Dagnes

1. Fa - ther, we love Thee, we praise Thee, we a - dore Thee.
2. Je - sus,
3. Spir - it,

Glo - ri - fy Thy name in all the earth.

Glo - ri - fy Thy name, glo - ri - fy Thy name.

Glo - ri - fy Thy name in all the earth.

GOD CALLING YET! SHALL I NOT HEAR

50

Gerhard Tersteegen
Tr. Sarah Findlater

Henry K. Oliver

1. God calling yet! - shall ___ I not hear?
   Earth's pleas-ures shall I still hold dear?
   Shall life's swift pass-ing years ___ all fly,
   And still my soul in slum-bers lie?

2. God calling yet! - shall ___ I not rise?
   Can I His lov-ing voice de-spise,
   And base-ly His kind care ___ re-pay?
   He calls me still; can I de-lay?

3. God calling yet - and ___ shall He knock
   And I my heart still clos-er lock?
   He still is wait-ing to ___ re-ceive,
   And shall I dare His Spir-it grieve?

4. God calling yet! - and ___ shall I give live?
   No heed, but still in bond-age live?
   I wait, but He does not ___ for-sake;
   He calls me still: My heart, a-wake!

5. Ah, yield Him all; in Him confide:
   Where but with Him doth peace abide?
   Break loose, let earthly bonds be riven,
   And let the spirit rise to heav'n!

6. God calling yet! - I cannot stay;
   My heart I yield without delay:
   Vain world, farewell! from thee I part;
   The voice of God hath reached my heart!

51 GREAT AND WONDERFUL

Rev. 15:3-4

Words and Music by
Stuart Dauermann

glo - ri - fy Thy___ name, O Lord?___

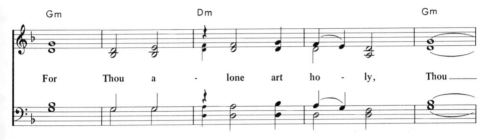

For Thou a - lone art ho - ly, Thou___

Coda

___ a - lone.___ men.___

D.C. al Coda

GOD IS SO GOOD

52

African melody

1. God is so good, God is so good, God is so good He's so good to me.

2. He cares for me___ 3. I'll do His will___ 4. He loves me so___

5. He answers prayer———

53 GREAT IS THE LORD

Psalm 48:1

Robert Ewing

Great is the Lord and great-ly to be praised.___ In the cit-y of our God, in the moun-tain of His ho-li-ness.

Beau-ti-ful for sit - u - a - tion,___ the joy of the whole earth,

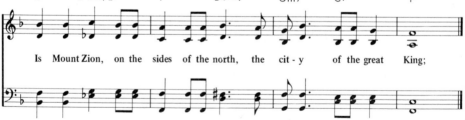

Is Mount Zion, on the sides of the north, the cit-y of the great King;

GROWING TOGETHER 54

Bob Laurent, Ralph Hunt, Kathy Brawley,
Pam Murphy and Mark Johnson

2. I'm waiting for the day, I can look at Him and say;
"Father, I thank you for your love."
CHORUS

3. It's in dying that we live, by giving we receive,
and growing become children of the light and the day.
CHORUS

55 GREAT IS THY FAITHFULNESS

Thomas Chisholm

William Runyan

1. "Great is Thy faith - ful - ness," O God my Fa - ther,
2. Sum - mer and win - ter, and spring - time and har - vest,
3. Par - don for sin and a peace that en - dur - eth,

There is no shad - ow of turn - ing with Thee;
Sun, moon and stars in their cours - es a - bove,
Thy own dear pres - ence to cheer and to - guide;

Thou chang - est not, Thy com - pas - sions, they fail not;
Join with all na - ture in man - i - fold wit - ness
strength for to - day and bright hope for to - mor - row,

As Thou hast been Thou for - ev - er wilt be.
To Thy great faith - ful - ness, mer - cy and love.
Bless - ings all mine, with ten thou - sand be - side!

"Great is Thy faith-ful-ness! Great is Thy faith-ful-ness!"
Morn-ing by morn-ing new mer-cies I see;
All I have need-ed Thy hand hath pro-vid-ed
"Great is Thy faith-ful-ness," Lord, un-to me!

THE B-I-B-L-E

56

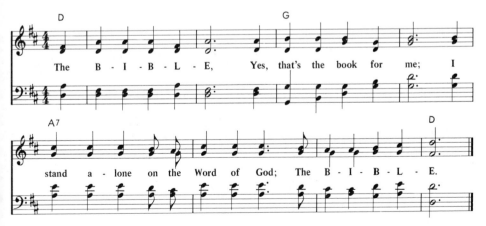

The B-I-B-L-E, Yes, that's the book for me; I
stand a-lone on the Word of God; The B-I-B-L-E.

57 HALLOWED BE THY NAME

Adapted from Matt. 6:9-13

Traditional West Indian Melody
Arr. by Lyndell Leathermann

HE GAVE ME BEAUTY FOR ASHES 58

Adapted from Isaiah 61:3

Unknown
Arr. by Tom Fettke

He gave me beau - ty for ash - es, the oil of joy for mourn - ing, The gar - ment of praise for the spir - it of heav - i - ness; That we might be trees of right - eous - ness, the plant - ing of the Lord; That He might be glo - ri - fied.

59 THE TREES OF THE FIELD

Isaiah (Adapted by Steffi Geiser Rubin)

Stuart Dauermann
Arr. by Henry Wiens

You shall go out with joy — and be led forth with peace. — The moun-tains and the hills will break forth be - fore you; There'll be shouts of joy, — and all the trees of the field will clap, will clap their hands. — And all the trees of the

2nd time Fine

field will clap their hands, ___ The trees of the field will

clap their hands. ___ The trees of the field will clap their hands, ___

___ while you go out with joy. You shall go

HE IS LORD 60

Based on Phil. 2:11

Traditional

He is Lord, He is Lord! He is ris - en from the dead, and He is

Lord! Ev - 'ry knee shall bow, ev - 'ry tongue con - fess That Je - sus Christ is Lord.

61 HE LIVES

Words and Music by
A. H. Ackley

1. I serve a ris - en Sav - ior, he's in the world to -
2. In all the world a - round me I see his lov - ing
3. Re - joice, re - joice, O Chris - tian, lift up your voice and

day; I know that he is liv - ing, what - ev - er
care, And though my heart grows wea - ry I nev - er
sing E - ter - nal hal - le - lu - jahs to Je - sus

men may say; I see his hand of mer -
will de - spair; I know that he is lead -
Christ the King! The Hope of all who seek

cy, I hear his voice of cheer, And just the
ing, through all the storm - y blast, The day of
him, the Help of all who find, None oth - er

time I need him he's al - ways near.
his ap - pear - ing will come at last.
is so lov - ing, so good and kind. He

Bb(G)　　　　　Bb7(G7)　Eb(C)

lives, _____ he lives, _____ Christ Je - sus lives __ to -

Bb(G)　　　F7(D7)　　　　　Bb(G)　　　　C7(A7)

day! ___ He walks with me and talks with me a - long life's

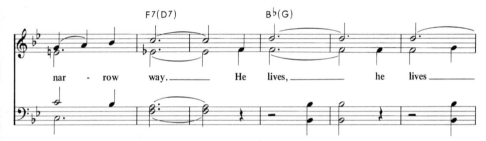

F7(D7)　　　Bb(G)

nar - row way. ___ He lives, _____ he lives ___

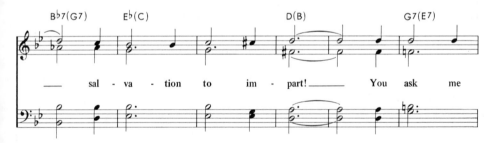

Bb7(G7)　Eb(C)　　　　　D(B)　　　　G7(E7)

___ sal - va - tion to im - part! ___ You ask me

C7(A7)　　　Eo(C#o) Bb/F(G/D) F7(D7)　　Bb(G)

how I know he lives? He lives with - in my heart. ___

62 HE RESTORETH MY SOUL

Words and Music by
Margaret Zilch

1. The Lord is my shep - herd I need him, When wea - ry and torn on life's way; His oil is a balm for my heal - ing, His rod and His staff are my stay.

2. In shad - y green pas - tures He feeds me, And there I shall rest in His care; By cool flow - ing wa - ters He leads me, And noth - ing can trou - ble me there.

3. His good - ness and mer - cy are with me, They fol - low me all my life through; With joy I will face each to - mor - row, Till heav - n's green pas - tures I view.

63 HE THE PEARLY GATES WILL OPEN

Fred Blom

Elsie Ahlwen
by W. Elmo Mercer

1. Love Di-vine, so great and won - drous, Deep and might - y, pure, sub - lime;
2. Like a dove when hunt - ed fright - ened, As a wound-ed fawn was I;
3. Love Di-vine, so great and won - drous, All my sins He then for - gave;
4. In life's e - ven - tide, at twi - light, At His door I'll knock and wait;

Com - ing from the heart of Je - sus, Just the same thro' tests of time.
Bro - ken-heart-ed yet He healed me, He will heed the sin - ner's cry.
I will sing His praise for - ev - er, For His blood, His pow'r to save.
By the pre-cious love of Je - sus. I shall en - ter heav-en's gate.

He the pearl - y gates will o - pen, So that I may en - ter in;

For he pur-chased my re - demp - tion, and for - gave me all my sin.

HEART SONG

64

Tim Newton

Je - sus is Lord.— Hear Him, all you peo - ple.— Je - sus is Lord.— and He

wants to be your King.——— Je - sus is Lord.— Hear Him, all you peo - ple—— just

call up-on His name and your heart will start to sing. Al - le - lu -jah Al - le - lu - jah!—

1. Je - sus is my Sav-ior and King.—— Al - le -   2. Je - sus is my Sav - ior and King. —

65 HE'S EVERYTHING TO ME

Words and Music by
Ralph Carmichael

66 GREAT IS THE LORD

Words and Music by
Michael W. Smith and Deborah D. Smith
Arr. by Henry Wiens

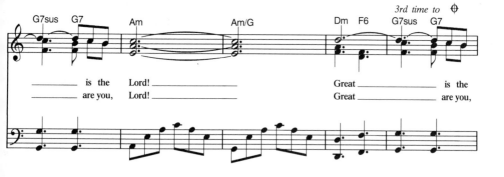

is the Lord! _____ Great _____ is the
are you, Lord! _____ Great _____ are you,

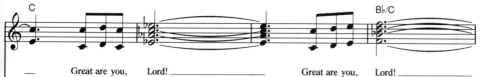

Lord! _____
Lord! _____

Lord! _____ Lord! _____

_ Great are you, Lord! _____ Great are you, Lord! _____

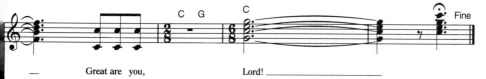

_ Great are you, Lord! _____

67 HEAVENLY FATHER, I APPRECIATE YOU

Unknown

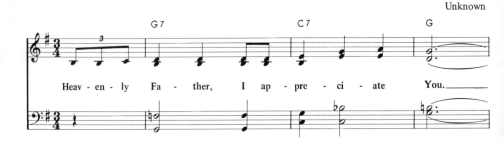

Heav - en - ly Fa - ther, I ap - pre - ci - ate You.

Heav-en-ly Fa - ther, I ap - pre - ci - ate You.

I love You, a - dore You, I bow down be -

fore You. Heav-en-ly Fa - ther, I ap - pre - ci - ate You.

HERE WE ARE

68

Words and Music by
Dallas Holm

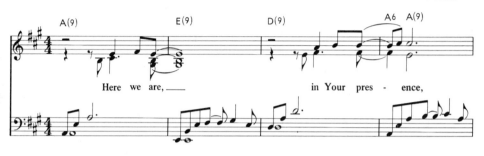

Here we are, _____ in Your pres - ence,

lift - ing ho - ly hands _____ to you. _____

Here we are, _____ prais - ing Je - sus

for the things _____ He's bro't us through. _____

69 HIS BANNER OVER ME IS LOVE

Adapted from Ps. 40:2;
Song 2:4; John 5:5
Anonymous

Unknown
Arr. by Lyndell Leatherman

1. I'm feast - ing__ at His__ ban- quet- ing__ ta - ble; His ban - ner o - ver me is love. I'm feast - ing__ at His__ ban - quet- ing__ ta - ble; His ban - ner o - ver me is love. I'm feast - ing__ at His__ ban - quet- ing__ ta - ble; His ban-ner o - ver me is love, His

2. He placed my__ feet on the firm__ foun - da - tion; His ban - ner o - ver me is love. He placed my__ feet on the firm__ foun - da - tion; His ban - ner o - ver me is love. He placed my__ feet on the firm__ foun - da - tion; His ban-ner o - ver me is love, His

3. __ He is the vine and__ we __ are the branch - es; His ban - ner o - ver me is love. __ He is the vine and__ we __ are the branch - es; His ban - ner o - ver me is love. __ He is the vine and__ we __ are the branch - es; His ban-ner o - ver me is love, His

4. I'm my beloved's and He is mine, His banner over me is love . . .

5. He lifts me up to the heavenly places, His banner over me is love . . .

6. One way to peace through the power of the cross, His banner over me is love. . . .

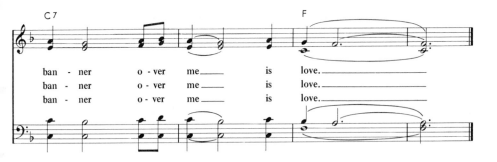

ban - ner o - ver me____ is love.____
ban - ner o - ver me____ is love.____
ban - ner o - ver me____ is love.____

BLESS THE LORD, O MY SOUL **70**

Adapted from Ps. 103:1

Unknown

Bless the Lord, O my soul; Bless the Lord, O my soul;

And all that is with - in me bless His ho - ly name.

71 HIS EYE IS ON THE SPARROW

Civilla D. Martin

Charles H. Gabriel.

1. Why should I feel dis - cour-aged, ___ Why should the shad - ows come, ___
2. "Let not your heart be troub-led," ___ His ten - der word I hear, ___
3. When - ev -er I am tempt-ed, ___ When - ev - er clouds a - rise, ___

Why should my heart be lone - ly. ___ And long for heav'n and home, ___ When
And rest - ing on His good- ness, ___ I lose my doubts and fears; ___ Tho'
When song gives place to sigh - ing, ___ When hope with - in me dies, ___ I

Je - sus is my por - tion? ___ My con - stant friend is He: ___ His
by the path He lead - eth, ___ But one step I may see: ___ His
draw the clos - er to Him, ___ From care He sets me free: ___ His

eye is on the spar - row, ___ And I know He watch - es me; ___ His
eye is on the spar - row, ___ And I know He watch - es me; ___ His
eye is on the spar - row, ___ And I know He cares - for me; ___ His

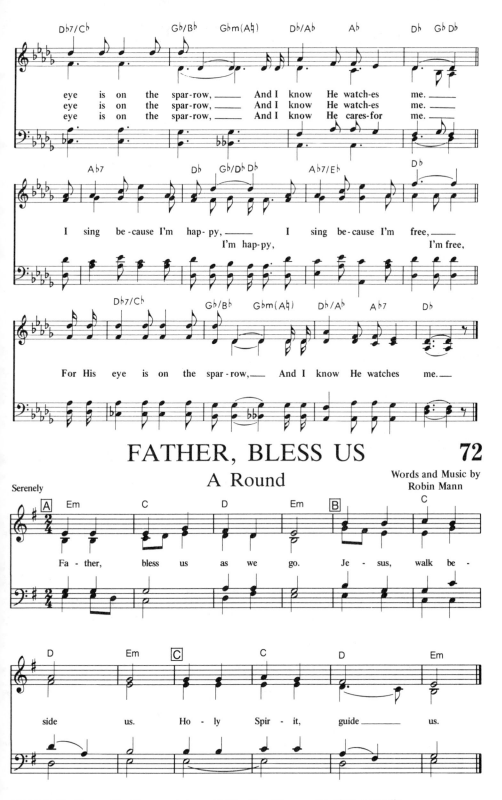

73 HIS NAME IS WONDERFUL

Audrey Mieir

His name is won-der-ful, His name is won-der-ful, His name is won-der-ful, Je-sus my Lord. He is the might-y King; Mas-ter of ev-'ry-thing; His name is won-der-ful,

Je - sus my Lord. He's the great shep - herd, the

rock of all a - ges. Al - might - y God is

He. _____ Bow down be - fore Him,

love and a - dore Him, His name is

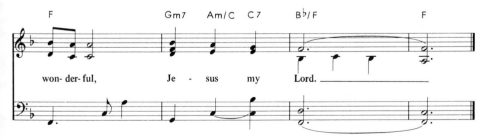

won- der- ful, Je - sus my Lord. _____

74   HOLY, HOLY

Words and Music by
Jimmy Owens

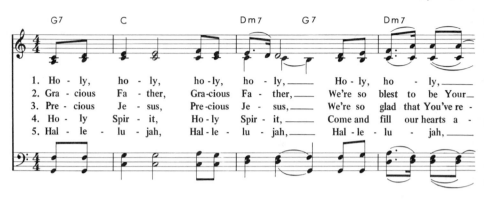

1. Ho - ly, ho - ly, ho - ly, ho - ly, _____ Ho - ly, ho - ly, _____
2. Gra - cious Fa - ther, Gra-cious Fa - ther, _____ We're so blest to be Your _____
3. Pre - cious Je - sus, Pre-cious Je - sus, _____ We're so glad that You've re -
4. Ho - ly Spir - it, Ho - ly Spir - it, _____ Come and fill our hearts a -
5. Hal - le - lu - jah, Hal - le - lu - jah, _____ Hal - le - lu - jah, _____

_____ Lord God Al - might - y; And we lift our hearts be - fore You as a
chil - dren, Gra - cious Fa - ther; And we lift our heads be - fore You as a
deemed us, Pre - cious Je - sus; And we lift our hands be - fore You as a
new, _____ Ho - ly Spir - it; And we lift our voice be - fore You as a
_____ Hal - le - lu - jah; And We lift our hearts be - fore You as a

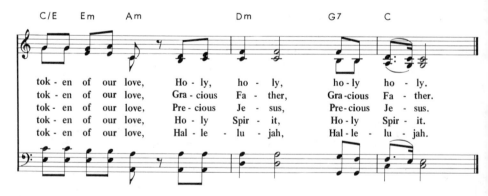

tok - en of our love, Ho - ly, ho - ly, ho - ly ho - ly.
tok - en of our love, Gra - cious Fa - ther, Gra-cious Fa - ther.
tok - en of our love, Pre - cious Je - sus, Pre-cious Je - sus.
tok - en of our love, Ho - ly Spir - it, Ho - ly Spir - it.
tok - en of our love, Hal - le - lu - jah, Hal - le - lu - jah.

CATCH THE VISION

Sandy Knoernschild

Arr. by John Rutter

1. O ev - 'ry - one of ea - ger heart, God's mes-sage to the world im -
2. All Christ-en - dom now hear His Word And let your hearts with - in be
3. Sons, rise to arms fear not the foe! With roy - al ban - ners for-ward
4. Let Je - sus' work your plea-sure be, Say, "Here am I, send me, send

part.
stirred. Catch the vi - sion of His mis - sion,
go.
me!"

Pro - claim how Je - sus lived and
To ev - 'ry na-tion, ev - 'ry
He sets His will be - fore your
Let not the an-swer heard from

Refrain

died That man might thus be jus - ti - fied;
place, Be thou a ves-sel of His grace.
eyes, And proves His law is good and wise.
you Be, "There is noth-ing I can do."

Catch the vi - sion of His

mis - sion, Catch the vi - sion of his mis - sion, Al - le - lu - ia!

76 HOLY SPIRIT, THOU ART WELCOME

Dottie Rambo
and David Huntsinger

Ho - ly Spir - it, Thou art wel - come in this

place. Ho - ly Spir - it, Thou art wel - come in this

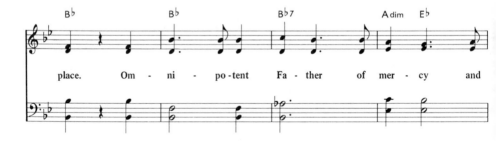

place. Om - ni - po - tent Fa - ther of mer - cy and

grace, Thou art wel - come in _____ this place. _____

Anonymous

78 HOW GREAT THOU ART

Stuart K. Hine

Swedish Melody

Slowly

1. O Lord my God! When I in awe-some won-der Con-sid-er
2. When through the woods and for-est glades I wan-der And hear the
3. And when I think that God, His son not spar-ing, Sent Him to
4. When Christ shall come with shout of ac-cla-ma-tion And take me

all the worlds Thy hands have made, __ I see the stars, I hear the roll-ing
birds sing sweet-ly in the trees; __ When I look down from loft-y moun-tain
die, I scarce can take it in; __ That on the cross, my bur-den glad-ly
home, what joy shall fill my heart! __ Then I shall bow in hum-ble ad-o-

thun-der, Thy pow'r through out the un-i-verse dis-played, __
gran-deur, And hear the brook and feel the gen-tle breeze; __
bear-ing, He bled and died to take a-way my sin; __
ra-tion And there pro-claim, my God, how great Thou art! __

Refrain

Then sings my soul, my Sav-ior God to Thee; __ How great Thou

A SONG OF PRAISE

79

Words and Music by John Worre

art, ____ how great Thou art! ____ Then sings my soul, my Sav - ior God to

Thee; ____ How great Thou art, ____ how great Thou art! ____

Sing a song of praise un - to the Lord. ____

Sing it out and Let your voice be heard. ____ He's the

King of kings up on the thrones, ____ He's the

Gladys I. Pearson

Vicki Vogel Schumidt

1. Oh, Lord, my God, Shin - ing in cre - a - tion
2. Oh, Lord, my God, King of ev - 'ry na - tion
3. Oh, Lord, my God, Spi - rit in - spir - a - tion

In moun - tains tall, In leaf, in air, in sea.
You came to earth To die to set me free.
My com - fort now And all the years to be.

Let ev - 'ry breeze Break forth in ad - u - la - tion
Let ev - 'ry voice Sing forth in ac - cla - ma - tion
Let ev - 'ry heart Bow down in a - dor - a - tion

And sing a hymn of joy to Thee! _____
And sing a hymn of joy to Thee! _____
And sing a hymn of joy to Thee! _____

* Arpeggiate left hand for accompaniment.

81   I AM JESUS' LITTLE LAMB

Henrietta L. von Hayn
Tr. Composite

Brüder Choral-Buch

I AM COVERED OVER

Unknown

I am cov-ered o-ver with the robe of right-eous-ness that Je-sus

gives to me,— (gives to me,)— I am cov-ered o-ver with the

pre-cious blood of Je-sus and He lives in me,— (lives in me,)—

Oh, what a joy it is to know, my Heav-en-ly Fa-ther loves me so, He

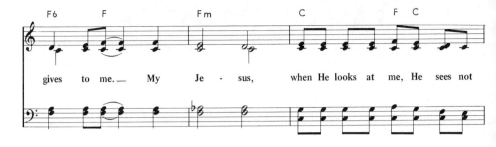

gives to me. — My Je - sus, when He looks at me, He sees not

what I used to be, but He sees Je - sus.

83 GREATER IS HE THAT IS IN ME

I John 4:4

Lanny Wolfe

Great - er is He — that is in me, Great - er is He — that is in me,

Great - er is He — that is in me than he that is in — the world!

I AM LOVED

84

Words and Music by
William J. Gaither
Arr. Henry Wiens

(1.2) I am loved, I am loved, I can risk lov-ing
(3) You are loved, You are loved, You can risk lov-ing

you, For the One ___ who knows me best loves me most.
too, For the One ___ who knows you best loves you most.

I am loved, you are loved, Won't you please take my
I am loved, we are loved, Won't you please take our

hand? We are free to love each oth-er We are loved!
hand? We are free to love each oth-er We are loved!

Chuck Girard
Arr. by Henry Wiens

Ad lib tempo with feeling

In the midst of my con - fu - sion, _ in the time _ of des-perate need, when I am think ing not too clear - ly _ a gen - tle voice does in -ter - cede. Slow down, slow down, be still _ be still, _ _ and wait _ on the Spir- it of _ the

Lord. _____ slow down _____ and hear _____ His voice _____ and know. _____ that He is

Ad lib tempo

God. _____ In the time __ of trib-u - la-tion __ when I'm feel-ing so un-sure when things are press ing in __ a bout me __ comes a gen-tle voice so still so pure. Slow God. _____

Fine

I HAVE CALLED YOU BY NAME 86

Words and Music by
Gloria Lien

"I have called you by name you are mine," says the Lord. I have called you by name Do not be a-fraid; I have called you by name. Be not a-fraid; I am your God, I am with you.

1. When you pass through deep wat - ers, I will be with you. Your
2. Do not lose hope or cour - age; I will be with you. My

trou - bles will not over — whelm you when you pass through the fire
pres - ence will be your strength each day when temp ta - tions o'er whelm

You will not be burned; The trials will not hurt you. I have
You will not give in; The trials will not hurt you. I have

D.S.

87

I HAVE DECIDED
TO FOLLOW JESUS

As Sung in Assam, India

Folk melody from India
Arr. N. J.

1. I have de - cid - ed _____ to fol - low Je - sus,_____
2. Tho no one join me,_____ still I will fol - low,_____
3. The world be - hind me,_____ the cross be - fore me,_____

_____ I have de - cid - ed _____ to fol - low Je - sus,_____
_____ Tho no one join me,_____ still I will fol - low,_____
_____ The world be - hind me,_____ the cross be - fore me,_____

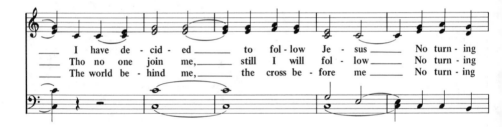

_____ I have de - cid - ed _____ to fol - low Je - sus _____ No turn - ing
_____ Tho no one join me,_____ still I will fol - low _____ No turn - ing
_____ The world be - hind me,_____ the cross be - fore me _____ No turn - ing

back, _____ no turn - ing back! _____
back, _____ no turn - ing back! _____
back, _____ no turn - ing back! _____

4. Take the whole world but give me Jesus, ... I'll follow Him, I'll follow Him.

I KNOW NOW

88

Words and Music by
Ray Hildebrand
Arr. by Henry Wiens

1. Born in a little man-ger low down in the back-side of Beth - le-hem one star - ry
2. Three wise men from a - far fol -lowed that star they knew who He

nite; Born to a mai - den named Ma - ry, car - pen - ter
was; Why did the shep- herds bow down with the sheep on the

Jo - seph that star - ry nite;
ground they knew who He was;

Some said He was nothin' but a Ba - by, born to a poor man that star - ry
Why did the King named He - rod kill all the ba - bies, he knew who He

nite; Some said He was God puttin' on skin and walk-in' a-mong
was; Why did the an - gels sing to the boy baby

FEED US NOW

89

Words and Music by
Robin Mann

Unhurried

1. Feed us now, Bread of life, In this ho - ly meal;
2. Piece of bread, glass of wine: Lord, this food is good!
3. God is here, O so near; Near - er than our thoughts.

Let us know your love a - new; We hun - ger _ for you.
Love and mer - cy come to us; Your prom - ise _ we trust.
Stay with us where - 'er we go; Lord, help us _ to grow.

Feed us now, Bread of life, Come and live with - in;
Piece of bread, glass of wine; Who can un - der - stand
God is here, O so near, In this heav - en's meal.

Let your peace be ours to - day, Lord Je - sus, we pray.
How His mer - cy works in these? Yet, Lord, we be - lieve.
May we al - ways feed on you - On the bread that is true.

Verses 1., 2. | Verse 3

90

I KNOW THAT
MY REDEEMER LIVES

Samuel Medley

John Hatton

1. I know that my Re - deem - er lives!
2. He lives to bless me with His love,
3. He lives to grant me rich sup - ply,
4. He lives to si - lence all my fears,
5. He lives all glo - ry to His name!

What com - fort this sweet sen - tence gives!
He lives to plead for me a - bove,
He lives to guide me with His eye,
He lives to wipe a - way my tears,
He lives, my Je - sus still the same;

He lives, He lives, Who once was dead,
He lives, my hun - gry soul to feed,
He lives to com - fort me when faint,
He lives to calm my trou - bled heart,
O the sweet joy this sen - tence gives:

He lives, my ev - er - liv - ing Head.
He lives to help in time of need.
He lives to hear my soul's com - plaint.
He lives all bless - ings to im - part.
I know that my Re - deem - er lives!

I LAY MY SINS ON JESUS

Horatius Bonar

Greek Melody

1. I lay my sins on Je - sus, The spot-less Lamb of God;
2. I lay my wants on Je - sus, All full- ness dwells in Him;
3. I long to be like Je - sus, Meek, lov - ing, low - ly, mild;

He bears them all and frees us From the ac - curs - ed load.
He heals all my dis - eas - es, He doth my soul re - deem.
I long to be like Je - sus, The Fa - ther's ho - ly Child.

I bring my guilt to Je - sus, To wash my crim - son stains.
I lay my griefs on Je - sus, My bur - dens and my cares:
I long to be with Je - sus, A - mid the heav'n - ly throng,

White in His blood most pre - cious, Till not a spot re - mains.
He from them all re - leas - es, He all my sor - rows shares.
To sing with saints His prais - es, To learn the an - gels' song.

92   I LOOK NOT BACK

Annie Johnson Flint

Oskar Ahnfelt

1. I look not back; God knows the fruit-less ef - forts, The wast - ed hours, the sin - ning, the re - grets. I leave them all with Him who blots the rec - ord, And gra - cious - ly for - gives, and then for - gets.

2. I look not for - ward; God sees all the fu - ture, The road that, short or long, will lead me home, And He will face with me its ev - 'ry tri - al, And bear for me the bur - dens that may come.

3. I look not round me; then would fears as - sail me, So wild the tu - mult of earth's rest-less seas, So dark the world, so filled with woe and e - vil, So vain the hope of com - fort and of ease. A - men.

4. I look not inward; that would make me wretched;
   For I have naught on which to stay my trust.
   Nothing I see save failures and shortcomings,
   And weak endeavors, crumbling into dust.

5. But I look up - into the face of Jesus,
   For there my heart can rest, my fears are stilled;
   And there is joy, and love, and light for darkness,
   And perfect peace, and every hope fulfilled.

I LOVE TO TELL THE STORY   93

Katherine Henkey

William G. Fischer

Chorus

I love to tell the sto -ry, 'Twill be my theme in glo - ry

To tell the old,, old sto - ry Of Je - sus and His love.

94 COME INTO HIS PRESENCE

Ps. 100:2, Rom. 10:9, Rev. 5:12

Unknown

Come in - to His presen - ce sing - ing

Al - le - lu - ia
Je - sus is Lord,
Wor - thy the Lamb,
Glo - ry to God,

Praise the Lord to - geth - er sing - ing

Al - le - lu - ia,
Je - sus is Lord,
wor - thy the Lamb,
glo - ry to God,

Al - le - lu - ia.
Je - sus is Lord.
wor - thy the Lamb.
glo - ry to God.

*can by sung as a four-part round.

I SAW THE LORD

95

Adapted from Isaiah 6:1, 3

Unknown
Arr. by Tom Fettke

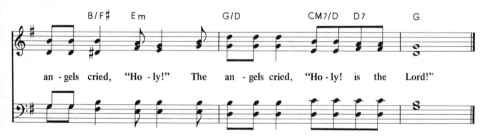

96   I WILL SING OF THE MERCIES

Adapted from Psalm 89:1

Unknown
Arr. by David Cole

I WILL SERVE THEE

William J. & Gloria Gaither

William J. Gaither

Slowly, with expression

I will serve Thee _____ be - cause I love Thee, _____ You have giv - en life to me; _____ I was noth - ing _____ be - fore You found me, _____ You have

IN HIS TIME

Adapted by D.B. from Eccles 3:11

Diane Ball

1. In His time (in His time), in His time (in His time),
2. In Your time (in Your time), in Your time (in Your time),

He makes all things beau - ti - ful in His time (in His time).
You make all things beau - ti - ful in Your time (in Your time).

Lord, please show me ev - 'ry day as You're teach - ing me Your way,
Lord, my life to You I bring; May each song I have to sing.

That You do just what You say in Your time (in Your time).
Be to You a love - ly thing in Your time (in Your time).

99 I WILL SING UNTO THE LORD

Exodus 15:1,2

Unknown

I will sing un-to the Lord— for He hath tri-umphed glo-rious-ly. — The

horse and rid-er thrown in-to the sea. I will sing un-to the Lord— for

He hath tri-umphed glo-rious-ly. — The horse and rid-er thrown in-to the sea. The

Lord, my God, my strength, my song has now be-come my vic-to-

ry. The Lord, my God, my strength, my song, has now be-come my vic-to-

ry. The Lord is God and I ___ will praise Him. My
Fa - ther is God and I ___ will ex - alt ___ Him. The Lord is God and
I ___ will praise Him. My Fa - ther is God and I ___ will ex - alt Him.

IT IS A GOOD THING
TO GIVE THANKS

100

Words and Music by
Judy Horner

Psalm 92:1, 4-5a

It is a good thing to give thanks unto the Lord; It is a good things to give
thanks un - to the Lord, and to sing prais - es un - to Thy Name, __ O most High. __

101   I'D RATHER HAVE JESUS

Rhea F. Miller

George Beverly Shea

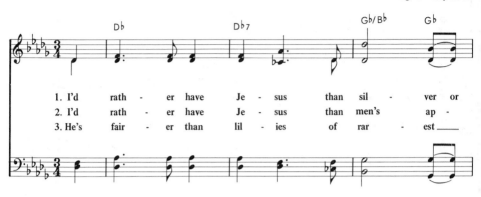

1. I'd rath - er have Je - sus than sil - ver or
2. I'd rath - er have Je - sus than men's ap -
3. He's fair - er than lil - ies of rar - est ____

gold, I'd rath - er be His than have rich - es un -
plause, I'd rath - er be faith - ful to His ____ dear
bloom, He's sweet - er than hon - ey from out ____ the

told; I'd rath - er have Je - sus than hous - es or
cause; I'd rath - er have Je - sus than world - wide
comb; He's all that my hun - ger - ing spir - it

102　IF MY PEOPLE WILL PRAY

Adapted by J.O. from II Chron 7:14

Jimmy Owens

103 IN THY PRESENCE, LORD

Words and Music by
Tom Elie

In Thy pres - ence, Lord, _____ In Thy pres - ence, Lord, _____

_____ I de - sire to be con - tin - ual - ly in Thy

pres - ence, Lord. _____ As I lift my hands be - fore You I lay

down all my am - bi - tions. I just de - sire to be con -

tin - ual - ly in Thy pres - ence, Lord.

INTO THY PRESENCE 104

Unknown
Titus 3:5

Unknown
Arr. by Lyndell Leatherman

In - to Thy pres - ence we come, we come;

Not by the works we have done, have done, ____

But by Thy grace, and Thy grace a - lone,

In - to Thy pres - ence we come, we come.

come. ____

105 IT IS NO SECRET
(What God Can Do)

Words and Music by
Stuart Hamblen

1. The chimes of time ring out the news; an-oth-er day is
(2. There) is no night, for in His light you'll nev-er walk a-

through Some-one slipped and fell. was that some-one
lone. Al-ways feel at home wher-ev-er you may

you? You may have longed for add-ed strength, your
roam. There is no power can con-quer you, while

cour-age to re-new. – Do not be dis-
God is on your side. Just take Him at His

106 IT IS WELL WITH MY SOUL

H. G. Spafford

Phillip P. Bliss

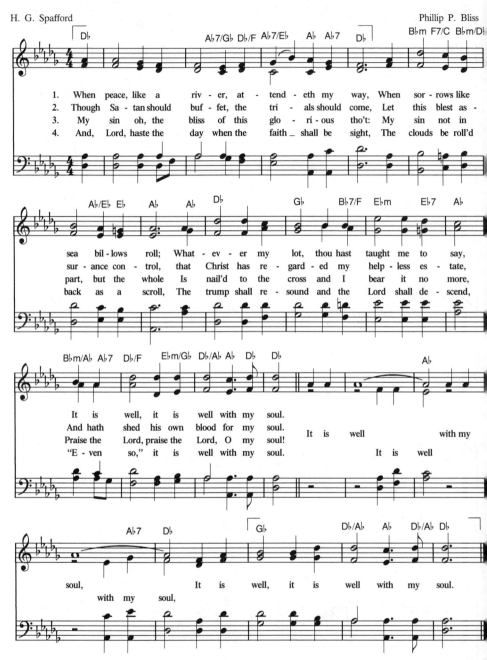

1. When peace, like a riv - er, at - tend - eth my way, When sor - rows like sea bil - lows roll; What - ev - er my lot, thou hast taught me to say, It is well, it is well with my soul. It is well, it is well with my soul.
2. Though Sa - tan should buf - fet, the tri - als should come, Let this blest as - sur - ance con - trol, that Christ has re - gard - ed my help - less es - tate, And hath shed his own blood for my soul.
3. My sin oh, the bliss of this glo - ri - ous tho't: My sin not in part, but the whole Is nail'd to the cross and I bear it no more, Praise the Lord, praise the Lord, O my soul!
4. And, Lord, haste the day when the faith shall be sight, The clouds be roll'd back as a scroll, The trump shall re - sound and the Lord shall de - scend, "E - ven so," it is well with my soul.

IT'S NO LONGER I
THAT LIVETH

Adapted from Gal. 2:20

Sally Ellis
Arr. by Lyndell Leatherman

It's no long - er I ____ that liv - eth, ____ But

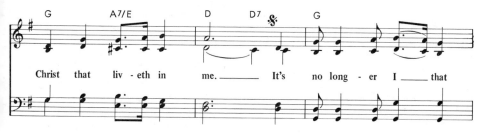

Christ that liv - eth in me. ____ It's no long - er I ____ that

liv - eth, ____ But Christ that liv - eth in me. He

Fine

lives, He lives, Je - sus is a - live in me.

D.S. al Fine

108 I'VE GOT PEACE LIKE A RIVER

Spiritual based on Isa. 48:18

Spiritual
Arr. by Lyndell Leatherman

1. I've got peace like a riv - er, I've got peace like a
2. I've got love like an o - cean, I've got love like an
3. I've got joy like a foun-tain, I've got joy like a

riv - er, I've got peace like a riv - er in my soul._____
o - cean, I've got love like an o - cean in my soul._____
foun-tain, I've got joy like a foun-tain in my soul._____

____ I've got peace like a riv - er, I've got peace like a
____ I've got love like an o - cean, I've got love like an
____ I've got joy like a foun-tain, I've got joy like a

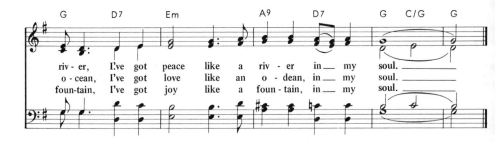

riv - er, I've got peace like a riv - er in__ my soul._____
o - cean, I've got love like an o - dean, in__ my soul._____
foun-tain, I've got joy like a foun - tain, in__ my soul._____

JEREMIAH 29:13

(And Ye Shall Seek Me)

109

Robert Rhodes

110   JEREMIAH 31:12

Adapted by Ray Rempt

The Ash Grove
English folk tune
Arr., Roger Nachtwey

There - fore＿ they shall come＿ and sing in the height of Zi - on and shall flow to - geth - er to the good - ness of the Lord. *For wheat and for wine, for oil and for the young,＿ for the young＿ of the flock＿ and of ＿ the herd. And their soul shall be＿ as a wa - tered gar - den, and they shall not sor - row an - y more＿ at all.

JESUS FED 5000

St. 1, K. E.
St. 2-5, Henry Ehlen

Kathy Ehlen

1. Je - sus fed five thou - sand peo - ple; All were seat - ed on the ground. First he broke the bread and blessed it, Then he passed it all a - round, Five loaves of bread and two lit - tle fish.

2. Je - sus gave a great big pic - nic To the peo - ple gath - ered there: Bread and fish were in the lunch box That a lit - tle boy did share, Five loaves of bread and two lit - tle fish.

3. Still so man - y folks are hun - gry; See how man - y you can feed. Try to be your broth - ers' keep - er; Share your bread with those in need. Five loaves of bread and two lit - tle fish.

112 FATHER WELCOMES

Words and Music by
Robin Mann

Smoothly

Fa - ther wel-comes all _ his chil- dren to _ his fam-'ly through his Son. _

Fa-ther giv-ing his _ sal - va- tion, Life _ for ev-er has been won.

won. 1. Lit - tle child - ren, come _ to me, for my king - dom is of these.
2. In the wa - ter, in _ the Word, in his prom - ise, be as - sured:
3. Let us dai - ly die _ to sin; let us dai - ly rise with him

D.C. al Fine

Life and _ love I have to _ give, Mer - cy _ for your sin.
Those who are bap - tized and be - lieves, Shall be _ born a - gain.
Walk in the love of Christ our _ Lord, Live in the peace of God.

©Kevin Mayhew LTD.
Rattlesden, Bury St. Edmunds,
Suffolk IP30 08Z. UNITED KINGDOM

JESUS, KEEP ME NEAR THE CROSS

113

Fanny J. Crosby

William Howard Doane

1. Je - sus, keep me near the Cross, There a pre - cious foun - tain
2. Near the Cross, a trembl - ing soul, Love and mer - cy found me;
3. Near the Cross! O Lamb of God, Bring its scen - es before me;
4. Near the Cross I'll watch and wait, Hop ing, trust - ing, ev - er,

Free to all a heal - ing stream, Flows from Cal - v'ry's moun - tain.
There the bright and morn - ing star Shed its beams a - round me.
Help me walk from day to day, With its shad - ows o'er me.
Till I reach the gold - en strand, Just be - yond the riv - er.

Chorus

In the Cross, in the Cross, Be my glo - ry ev - er;

Till my rap - tured soul shall find Rest be - yond the riv - er.

114 JESUS LOVES ME

Anna B. Warner, alt.

Wm. B. Bradbury

1. Je - sus loves me! This I know, for the Bi - ble tells me so:
2. Je - sus loves me! Loves me still, Tho' I'm ver - y weak and ill;
3. Je - sus loves me! He who died, Heav - en's gate to o - pen wide;
4. Je - sus loves me! He will stay Close be - side me all the way;

Lit - tle ones to Him be - long; They are weak but He is strong.
That I might from sin be free, Bled and died up - on the tree.
He will wash a - way my sin, Let His lit - tle child come in.
Thou hast bled and died for me, I will hence - forth live for thee.

Yes, Je - sus loves me! Yes, Je - sus loves me!

Yes, Je - sus loves me! The Bi - ble tells me so.

JESUS, NAME ABOVE ALL NAMES

115

Adapted by Naida Hearn from
Matt. 1:23; Phil. 2:5-11

Patricia Cain

1. Je - sus, name a - bove all names, beau-ti - ful Sav - ior, glo - ri - ous Lord, _____ Em - man - u - el, God is with us, bless-ed Re - deem - er, liv - ing Word.

2. Jesus, loving shepherd
   Vine of the branches, Son of God
   Prince of Peace, Wonderful counselor
   Lord of the universe, Light of the world.

3. Jesus, Way of salvation,
   King of kings, Lord of Lords,
   the way the truth, and the Life,
   Mighty creator, my Savior and friend.

116 JESUS, THOU ART HOLY

Unknown

1. Je - sus, Thou art ho - ly, the ho - ly Son of God, The
ho - ly Son of God, The ho - ly Son of God; Al - le - lu - ia to Thy
name, Al - le - lu - ia to Thy name, Al - le - lu - ia to Thy
name, Je - sus.

2. Jesus, thou art worthy, worthy to be praised . . .

3. Jesus, thou art Savior, Savior of the world

4. Jesus, thou art master, master of my heart . . .

PEOPLE NEED THE LORD   117

Greg Nelson and Phill McHugh
Arr. by Henry Wiens

Ev-'ry day they pass me by. I can see it in their eye; _
We are called to take His light to a world where wrong seems right; _

Emp - ty peo-ple filled with care, head-ed who knows where. _____
What could be too great a cost for shar-ing life with one who's lost.

On they go through _ pri - vate pain, liv-ing fear to fear. _____
Through His love our _____ hearts can feel all the grief they bear. _____

Laugh-ter hides the si - lent cries _ on-ly Je-sus hears. _
They must hear the words of life _ on-ly we can share. _

Peo-ple need the Lord. __ Peo-ple need the Lord. __

JOYFUL, JOYFUL, WE ADORE THEE

118

Henry Van Dyke

Arr. from Ludwig van Beethoven

1. Joy - ful, joy - ful, we a - dore Thee, God of glo - ry, Lord of love;
2. All Thy works with joy sur - round Thee, Earth and heav'n re - flect Thy rays,
3. Thou art giv - ing and for - giv - ing, Ev - er bless - ing, ev - er blest,
4. Mor - tals, join the might - y cho - rus Which the morn - ing stars be - gan;

Hearts un - fold like flow'rs be - fore Thee, Hail Thee as the sun a - bove.
Stars and an - gels sing a - round Thee, Cen - ter of un - bro - ken praise;
Well - spring of the joy of liv - ing, O - cean - depth of hap - py rest!
Fa - ther love is reign - ing o'er us, Broth - er - love binds man to man.

Melt the clouds of sin and sad - ness; Drive the dark of doubt a - way;
Field and for - est, vale and moun - tain, Flow - 'ry mead - ow flash - ing sea,
Thou our Fa - ther, Christ our Broth - er, All who live in love are Thine:
Ev - er sing - ing, march we on - ward, Vic - tors in the midst of strife;

Giv - er of im - mor - tal glad - ness, Fill us with the light of day!
Chant - ing bird and flow - ing foun - tain, Call us to re - joice in Thee.
Teach us how to love each oth - er, Lift us to the Joy Di - vine.
Joy - ful mu - sic lifts us sun - ward In the tri - umph song of life.

119   JUST AS I AM

Charlotte Elliott

Wm. B. Bradbury

1. Just as I am, without one plea, But

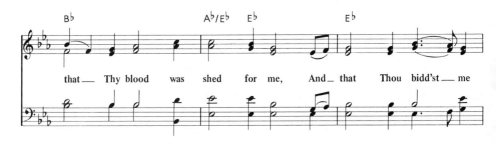

that Thy blood was shed for me, And that Thou bidd'st me

come to Thee, O Lamb of God, I come! I come!

2. Just as I am, and waiting not,
To rid my soul of one dark blot,
To Thee whose blood can cleanse each spot,
O Lamb of God, I come! I come!

3. Just as I am, tho' tossed about
With many a conflict, many a doubt,
Fightings and fears within, without,
O Lamb of God, I come! I come!

4. Just as I am, poor, wretched, blind;
Sight, riches, healing of the mind,
Yea, all I need, in Thee to find,
O Lamb of God, I come! I come!

5. Just as I am, Thou wilt receive,
Wilt welcome, pardon, cleanse, relieve;
Because Thy promise I believe,
O Lamb of God, I come! I come!

LEAD ON, O KING ETERNAL 120

Ernest W. Schurtleff

Henry Smart

1. Lead on, O King E - ter - nal, The day of march has come; Hence
2. Lead on, O King E - ter - nal, Till sin's fierce war shall cease, And
3. Lead on, O King E - ter - nal, We fol - low, not with fears; For

forth in fields of con - quest Thy tents shall be our home. Thro'
ho - li - ness shall whis - per The sweet A - men of peace; For
glad - ness breaks like morn - ing Where - 'er Thy face ap - pears; Thy

days of prep - a - ra - tion Thy grace has made us strong, And
not with swords loud clash - ing, Nor roll of stir - ring drums; With
cross is lift - ed o'er us; We jour - ney in its light: The

now, O King E - ter - nal, We lift our bat - tle song.
deeds of love and mer - cy, The heaven - ly king - dom comes.
crown a waits the con - quest; Lead on, O God of might.

121 LET ALL THAT IS WITHIN ME

Adapted from Ps. 103:1; Rev. 5:12

Unknown
Arr. by Lyndell Leatherman

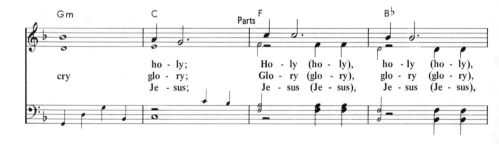

LET OUR PRAISE TO YOU
BE AS INCENSE

Words and Music by
Brent Chambers

join the hosts of an - gels, and pro - claim to - geth - er Your

ho-li - ness. ___ Let our ___ Ho - ly, ho - ly,

ho - ly, ho - ly is the Lord.

123 FOR GOD SO LOVED THE WORLD

Frances Townsend

Alfred B. Smith

1. For God so loved the world He gave His on - ly Son To
2. Some day He's com - ing back What glo - ry that will

die on Cal -v'ry's tree, From sin to set me free;

be! Won - der - ful His love to me. ___

LET THE HILLS NOW SING FOR JOY

124

Ps. 98

Gary Johnson

2nd Part (optional)

O, let the hills

Melody

1. O let the hills now sing for
2. Sing to the Lord a brand new
3. Break forth in joy with hap - py

now sing for joy! And let the

joy! And let the sea
song! For He has done
song! Praise to the Lord

sea now roar its praise!

now roar its praise! And let the
glo - ri - ous deeds! His own right
in sym - pho - ny! Let all the

LET THE WORDS
OF MY MOUTH

Psalm 19:14

John Worre

Let the words of my mouth, and the
med - i - ta - tions of my heart, be ac - cep - ta - ble in Thy sight,
oh Lord, oh Lord, Let the
(Lord) oh Lord, my strength, and my re -
deem - - er. oh (er).

126 LET US BREAK BREAD TOGETHER

Traditional Spiritual

1. Let us break bread to-geth-er on our knees, _____ Let us break bread to-geth-er on our knees; _____ When I fall on my knees with my face to the ris - ing sun, O_____ Lord, have mer-cy on me! _____

2. Let us drink wine (or the cup) together . . .   3. Let us bow 'round the alter . . .

4. Let us praise God together . . . .

LET US PRAY

127

Words and Music by
Ray Hildebrand

Let us pray un-to the Lord in u-ni-ty and one ac-cord. Take the hand of the one stand-ing by your side, And let's con-fess un-to the Lord that we have failed and fal-len short; And He will hear us, __ and He will help us. __ Let us pray. __

128 LET'S JUST PRAISE THE LORD

William J. and Gloria Gaither

William J. Gaither

John 12:32

Unknown

1. Let's lift up Je - sus. Let's lift up Je - sus. Lift Him up for e - ter - ni - ty. He said, "If I be lift - ed up from the earth, I will draw all men un - to me."

2. Let's lift Him higher. Let's lift Him higher.
Lift Him up for eternity.
He said,"If I be lifted up from the earth,
I will draw all men unto me."

130 LIFT HIGH THE CROSS

George W. Kitchin, Michael R. Newbolt

Sydney H. Nicholson

Refrain

Lift high the cross, the love of Christ pro-claim Till all the world a-dore his sa-cred name.

1. Come Chris-tains, fol-low where our cap-tain trod, Our king vic-to-rious, Christ, the Son of God.
2. Led on their way by this tri-um-phant sign, The hosts of God in con-qu'ring ranks com-bine.
3. All new-born sol-diers of the Cru-ci-fied Bear on their brows the seal of him who died.
4. O Lord, once lift-ed on the glo-rious tree, As thou hast prom-ised, draw us all to thee.

5. So shall our song of triumph ever be:
Praise to the Crucified for victory! Refrain

LIFT UP YOUR HEADS, OH YE GATES

131

Psalm 24

132 LORD, SPEAK TO ME THAT I MAY SPEAK

Frances R. Havergal

Robert Schumann

1. Lord, speak to me, that I may speak
   In liv-ing ech-oes of Thy tone;
   As Thou hast sought, so let me seek
   Thy err-ing chil-dren lost and lone.

2. O lead me, Lord, that I may lead
   The wan-d'ring and the wav-'ring feet;
   O feed me, Lord, that I may feed
   Thy hun-g'ring ones with man-na sweet.

3. O teach me, Lord, that I may teach
   The pre-cious things Thou dost im-part;
   And wing my words, that they may reach
   Thy hid-den depths of many a heart.

4. O fill me, with Thy ful-ness, Lord,
   Un-til my ver-y heart o'er-flow
   In kind-ling thought and glow-ing word,
   Thy love to tell, Thy praise to show.

LOVE, LOVE

133

Arr. Roger Nachtwey

Round: Successive voices enter after each two measures.

Em D Em B Em D

1. Love, love, love, love, Chris - tians, this
2. Glo - ry to God in the high - est, Glo - ry to God in the
3. King of __ kings and __ Lord of lords, King of kings for -
4. Praise the Fa - ther, __ praise the Son, __ Praise the Spir - it, __

Em B Em D Em B

is your call. Love your neigh - bor as your - self, For
high - est; Peace on earth, good will towards men.
ev - er - more. King of kings and Lord of __ lords,
three in __ one. Praise the Fa - ther, praise the __ Son,

Em D Em B*

God loves __ all. __
Glo - ry to God in the high - est.
King of __ kings for - ev - er.
Praise the __ Spir - it, Three in One.

* Omit last time.

134   LOVE, LOVE, LOVE

Herbert Brokering

Lois Brokering

       * 2; Peace, peace, peace!   3. Joy, joy, joy!
                4. Me, me, me!   5. You, you, you!

MAJESTY

Words and Music by
Jack Hayford

Maj - es - ty, _____ wor-ship His maj - es - ty. _____ Un - to

Je - sus be all glo - ry pow-er and praise. _____

Maj - es - ty, _____ king-dom auth - or - i - ty _____ flow from His
Maj - es - ty, _____ wor-ship His maj - es - ty, _____ Je - sus, who

throne un - to His own who His an - them raise. _____ So ex -
died, now glo - ri - fied, _____ King of all kings. _____

Fine

D.S. al Fine

136 WORTHY IS THE LAMB

Words and Music by
Don Wyrtzen

137 MAKE ME A CAPTIVE, LORD

George Matheson

George William Martin
Arr. Arthur S. Sullivan

In moderate time

1. Make me a cap - tive, Lord, And then I shall be free;
2. My heart is weak and poor Un - til it mas - ter find;

Force me to ren - der up my sword, And I shall con - queror be.
It has no spring of ac - tion sure, It var - ies with the wind.

I sink in life's a - larms When by my - self I stand;
It can - not free - ly move Till thou hast wrought its chain;

Im - pris - on me with - in thine arms, And strong shall be my hand.
En - slave it with thy matchless love, And death - less it shall reign. A - men.

3. My power is faint and low
   Till I have learned to serve;
   It wants the needed fire to glow,
   It wants the breeze to nerve;
   It cannot drive the world
   Until itself be driven;
   Its flag can only be unfurled
   When thou shalt breathe from heaven.

4. My will is not my own
   Til thou hast made it thine;
   If it would reach a monarch's throne
   It must its crown resign;
   It only stands unbent
   Amid the clashing strife,
   When on thy bosom it has leant
   And found in thee its life. Amen.

MAKE ME LIKE YOU

Words and Music by
Jimmy and Carol Owens

Lord, make me ____ like You. Please make me like You. You are a ser - vant. Make me one, too. Oh Lord, I am will - ing. Do what You must do ____ to make me like You, ___ Lord. Just make me like You.

139 MY FAITH LOOKS UP TO THEE

Ray Palmer

Lowell Mason

MAKE THIS CHILD YOURS 140

Words and Music by
Gloria Lien

Take this child, Make her yours, Make her part of your fam - i - ly. From your
(him)   (him)

love she has come; In your love may she al - ways be. Let not
(he)   (he)

time or ___ age take her far from your fam - i - ly. May she
(him)   (he)

grow; may she stay ___ close to you. ___ To
(he)

you, _____ dear Lord, we praise thee _____ for the

bless - ings of your perfect gift _____ To

you, _____ dear Lord, our heart - felt thanks, we lift our

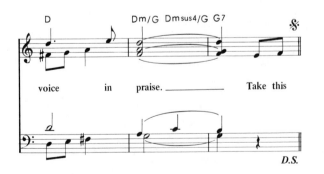

voice in praise. _____ Take this

you.

MARY'S LITTLE BOY CHILD   141

Words and Music by
Jester Hairston

ev - er-more   be - cause of   Christ-mas   day.   2. While
ev - er-more   be - cause of   Christ-mas   3. Now

D.S. al Coda

day.

142   WE WILL GLORIFY

Twila Paris
Arr. Henry Wiens

1. We   will   glo - ri - fy   the   King   of   Kings;   We   will
2. Hal - le - lu - jah   to   the   King   of   Kings;   Hal - le -
3. Lord   Je - ho - vah   reigns   in   maj - es - ty;   We   will

glo - ri - fy   the   Lamb;   We   will   glo - ri - fy   the
lu - jah   to   the   Lamb;   Hal - le - lu - jah   to   the
bow   be - fore   His   throne;   We   will   wor - ship   Him   in

Lord   of   Lords,   Who ___   is   the   great   I   Am.
Lord   of   Lords,   Who ___   is   the   great   I   Am.
right - eous - ness;   We   will   wor - ship   Him   a - lone.

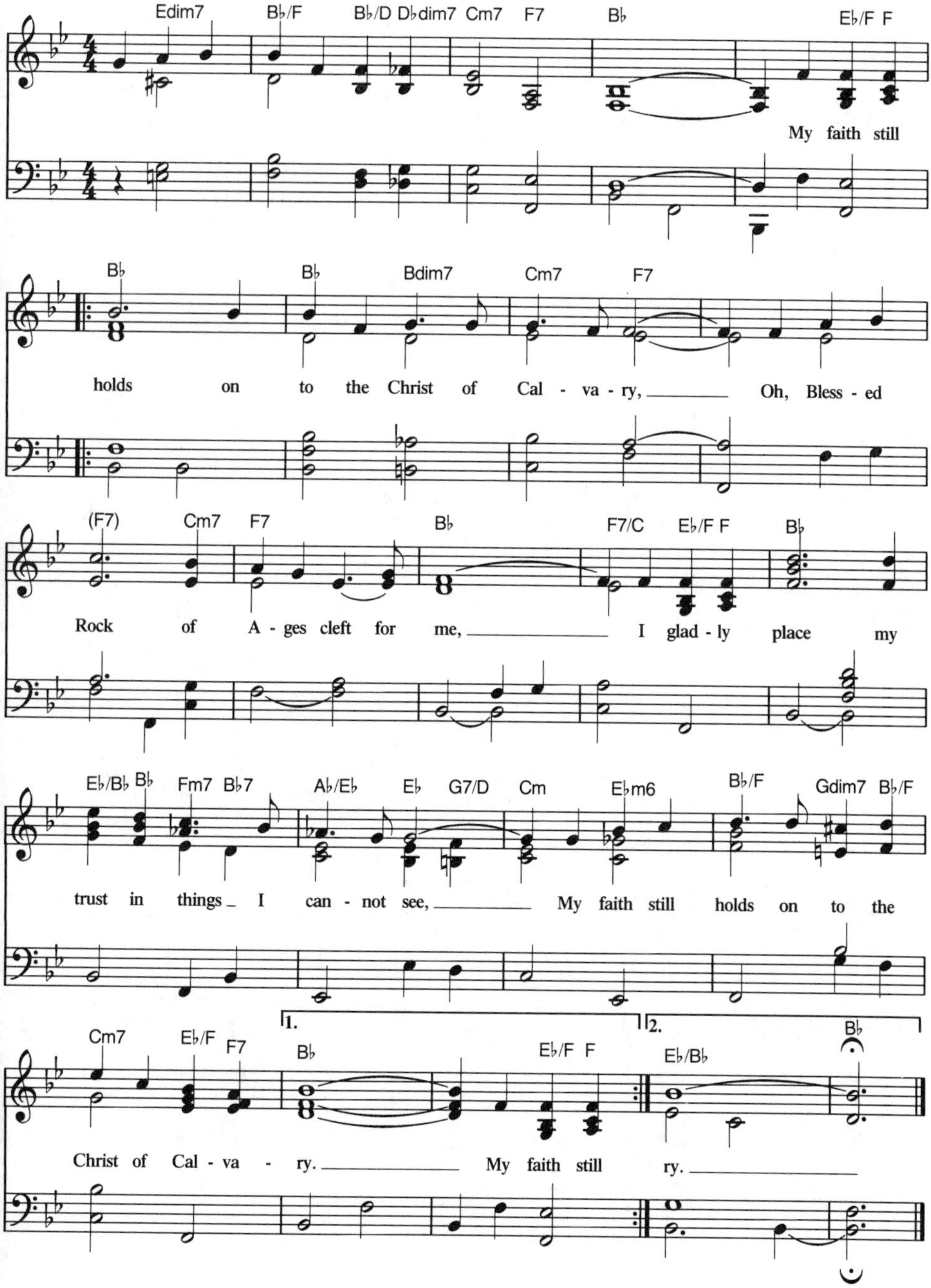

MY FAITH STILL HOLDS

William J. and Gloria Gaither

William J. Gaither

Edim7 B♭/F B♭/D D♭dim7 Cm7 F7 B♭ E♭/F F
My faith still
B♭ B♭ Bdim7 Cm7 F7
holds on to the Christ of Cal - va - ry, Oh, Bless - ed
(F7) Cm7 F7 B♭ F7/C E♭/F F B♭
Rock of A - ges cleft for me, I glad - ly place my
E♭/B♭ B♭ Fm7 B♭7 A♭/E♭ E♭ G7/D Cm E♭m6 B♭/F Gdim7 B♭/F
trust in things I can - not see, My faith still holds on to the
1. 2.
Cm7 E♭/F F7 B♭ E♭/F F E♭/B♭ B♭
Christ of Cal - va - ry. My faith still ry.

144 MY JESUS, I LOVE THEE

Anonymous

Adoniram J. Gordon

1. My Je - sus, I love ___ Thee, I know Thou art mine,
2. I love Thee be - cause ___ Thou hast first lov - ed me,
3. I'll love Thee in life, ___ I will love Thee in death,
4. In man - sions of glo - ry and end - less de - light,

For Thee all the fol - lies of sin I re - sign;
And pur - chased my par - don on Cal - va - ry's tree;
And praise Thee as long as Thou lend - est me breath;
I'll ev - er a - dore Thee in heav - en so bright;

My gra - cious Re - deem - er, my Sav - ior art Thou, ___
I love Thee for wear - ing the thorns ___ on Thy brow, ___
And say when the death - dew lies cold ___ on my brow, ___
I'll sing with the glit - ter - ing crown ___ on my brow, ___

If ev - er I loved ___ Thee, my Je - sus, 'tis now.
If ev - er I loved ___ Thee, my Je - sus, 'tis now.
If ev - er I loved ___ Thee, my Je - sus, 'tis now.
If ev - er I loved ___ Thee, my Je - sus, 'tis now.

MY TRIBUTE

145

Words & Music by
Andrae Crouch

To God, be the glo - ry, to God, be the glo - ry, To God be the glo - ry, for the things He has done! With His blood He has saved me, With His pow'r He has raised me; To God be the glo - ry, For the things __ He has done! done. Just let me

Optional ending

Fine

146 LORD, WE PRAISE YOU

Otis Skillings

NEW TESTAMENT SONG 147

Source Unknown

Mat - thew, Mark and Luke and John, Acts, Ro - mans, First and Sec-ond Cor -

in - thi - ans, Ga - la - tians, E-phe sians, Phil - ip - pi- ans, Col - os-sians,

First and Sec-ond Thes-sa - lo - ni-ans, First Tim- o- thy, Sec - ond Tim-o -thy,

Ti - tus, Phi - le - mon, He - brews, James,___ First Pe - ter

Sec - ond Pe - ter, three Johns, Jude and Re - vel - a - tion.

148 O LOVE THAT WILT NOT LET ME GO

George Matheson

Albert L. Peace

1. O Love that wilt not let me go, I rest my wea - ry soul in Thee; I give Thee back the life I owe, That in Thine o - cean depths its flow May rich - er, full - er be.

2. O Light that fol - l'west all my way, I yield my flick - 'ring torch to Thee; My heart re - stores its bor - rowed ray, That in Thy sun - shine's blaze its day May bright - er, fair - er be.

3. O Joy that seek - est me thro' pain, I can - not close my heart to Thee; I trace the rain - bow thro' the rain, And feel the prom - ise is not vain That morn shall tear - less be.

4. O Cross that lift - est up my head, I dare not ask to fly from Thee; I lay in dust life's glo - ry dead, And from the ground there blos - soms red life's that shall end - less be.

NO ONE EVER CARED FOR ME LIKE JESUS   149

Words and Music by
C. F. Weigle

1. I would love to tell you what I think of Je - sus Since I found in Him a friend so strong and true; I would tell you how He changed my life com-plete - ly, He did some-thing that no oth - er friend could do.

2. All my life was full of sin when Je - sus found me, All my heart was full of mis - er - y and woe; Je - sus plac'd His strong and lov - ing arms a - bout me, And He led me in the way I ought to go.

3. Ev - 'ry day He comes to me with new as - sur - ance, More and more I un - der - stand His words of love; But I'll nev - er know just why He came to save me, Till some day I see His bless - ed face a - bove,

No one ev - er cared for me like Je - sus, There's no oth - er friend so kind as He; No one

else could take the sin and dark - ness   from me,   O how much He cared for   me.

150   I HAVE THE JOY

Arr. by H. D. L.

1. I   have   the   joy,   joy,   joy,   joy,   down in   my heart,
2. I   have   the   peace that pass - es   un - der - stand-ing,   down in   my heart,
3. I   have   the   love of   Je - sus,   love of   Je - sus,   down in   my heart,

Down in   my heart,   down in   my heart;   I   have   the   joy,   joy,
Down in   my heart,   down in   my heart;   I   have   the   peace that pass - es
Down in   my heart,   down in   my heart;   I   have   the   love of   Je - sus,

joy,   joy,   down in   my heart,   Down in   my heart   to   stay.
un - der - stand - ing,   down in   my heart,   Down in   my heart   to   stay.
love of   Je - sus,   down in   my heart,   Down in   my heart   to   stay.

* "Where!"

OH, FOR A
THOUSAND TONGUES

Charles Wesley

William Gardiner

1. Oh, for a thou - sand tongues to sing My
2. My, gra - cious Mas - ter and my God, As -
3. Je - sus, the name that charms our fears, That
4. He breaks the pow'r of can - celed sin, He
5. Hear him, ye deaf; his praise, ye dumb, Your

great Re - deem - er's praise, The glo - ries of my
sist me to pro - claim, To spread through all the
bids our sor - rows cease, Tis mu - sic in the
sets the pris - 'ner free, His blood can make the
loos - ened tongues em - ploy; Ye blind, be - hold your

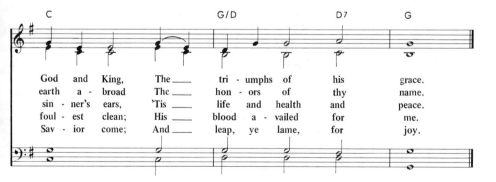

God and King, The___ tri - umphs of his grace.
earth a - broad The___ hon - ors of thy name.
sin - ner's ears, 'Tis___ life and health and peace.
foul - est clean; His___ blood a - vailed for me.
Sav - ior come; And___ leap, ye lame, for joy.

152 OH, HOW I LOVE JESUS

Words and Music by
Frederick Whitfield

2. To me, He is so wonderful (3 times)
   Because He first loved me.

3. And now, He is my righteousness (3 times)
   Because He first loved me.

OH, HOW HE LOVES YOU AND ME

153

Adapted from John 15:13; I John 4:9-10

Kurt Kaiser

1. Oh, how He loves you and me; Oh, how He loves you and me. He gave His life — what more could He give? — Oh, how He loves you; Oh, how He loves me; Oh, how He loves you and me.

2. Je - sus to Cal - v'ry did go, His love for sin - ners to show. What He did there — brought hope from de - spair. —

154 OPEN MINE EYES

Clarence A. Johnson

1. O - pen mine eyes, O Lord, O - pen mine eyes;
2. O - pen mine eyes, O Lord, O - pen mine eyes;

In - to my dark - ened heart Let Thy light a - rise.
Thy Word and Sac - ra - ment Let me ne'er de - spise!

Show me my - self, O Lord, Show me Thy - self, O Lord,
Thou art the Way, O Lord, Thou art the Truth, O Lord,

Show me Thy truth, O Lord, O - pen mine eyes!
Thou art the Life, O Lord, O - pen mine eyes!

ON EAGLE'S WINGS 155

Words and Music by
Michael Joncas

156   I AM A "C"

Source Unknown

OPEN OUR EYES

157

Words & Music by
Bob Cull

158 I LOVE YOU, LORD

Words & Music by
John Worre

OPEN MY EYES, THAT I MAY SEE

159

Words and Music by
Chas. H. Scott

1. O-pen my eyes, that I may see Glimps-es of truth Thou hast for me;
2. O-pen my ears, that I may hear Voi-ces of truth Thou send-est clear;
3. O-pen my mouth, and let me bear Glad-ly the warm truth ev-'ry-where;

Place in my hands the won-der-ful key That shall un-clasp, and set me free.
And while the wave-notes fall on my ear, Ev-'ry-thing false will dis-ap-pear.
O-pen my heart, and let me pre-pare Love with Thy chil-dren thus to share.

Si-lent-ly now I wait for Thee, Read-y, my God, Thy will to see;
Si-lent-ly now I wait for Thee, Read-y, my God, Thy will to see;
Si-lent-ly now I wait for Thee, Read-y, my God, Thy will to see;

O-pen my eyes, il-lu-mine me, Spir-it di-vine!
O-pen my ears, il-lu-mine me, Spir-it di-vine!
O-pen my heart, il-lu-mine me, Spir-it di-vine!

160 PASSED THRU THE WATERS

Words and Music by
Richard Avery
Donald Marsh

OUR GOD REIGNS

161

Isaiah 52:7,53

Words & Music by Leonard E. Smith, Jr.

Capo 1, Play A

1. How love-ly on the moun-tains are the feet of Him
2. He had no state - ly form, He had no maj - es - ty,
3. It was our sin and guilt that bruised and wound - ed Him.
4. Meek as a lamb that's led out to the slaugh - ter house,
5. Out from the tomb He came with grace and ma - je - sty,

who brings good news, good news,
that we should be drawn to Him.
It was our sin that brought Him down.
Dumb as a sheep before its shearer,
He is al - ive, He is alive.

an - nounc - ing peace, pro - claim - ing news of hap - pi - ness
He was des - pised and we took no ac - count of Him,
When we like sheep had gone a - stray, our shep - herd came
His life ran down up on the ground like pour - ing rain,
God loves us so, see here His hands, His feet, His side,

OUR NEW SONG OF PRAISE 162

Adapted from Ps. 40

David Steele

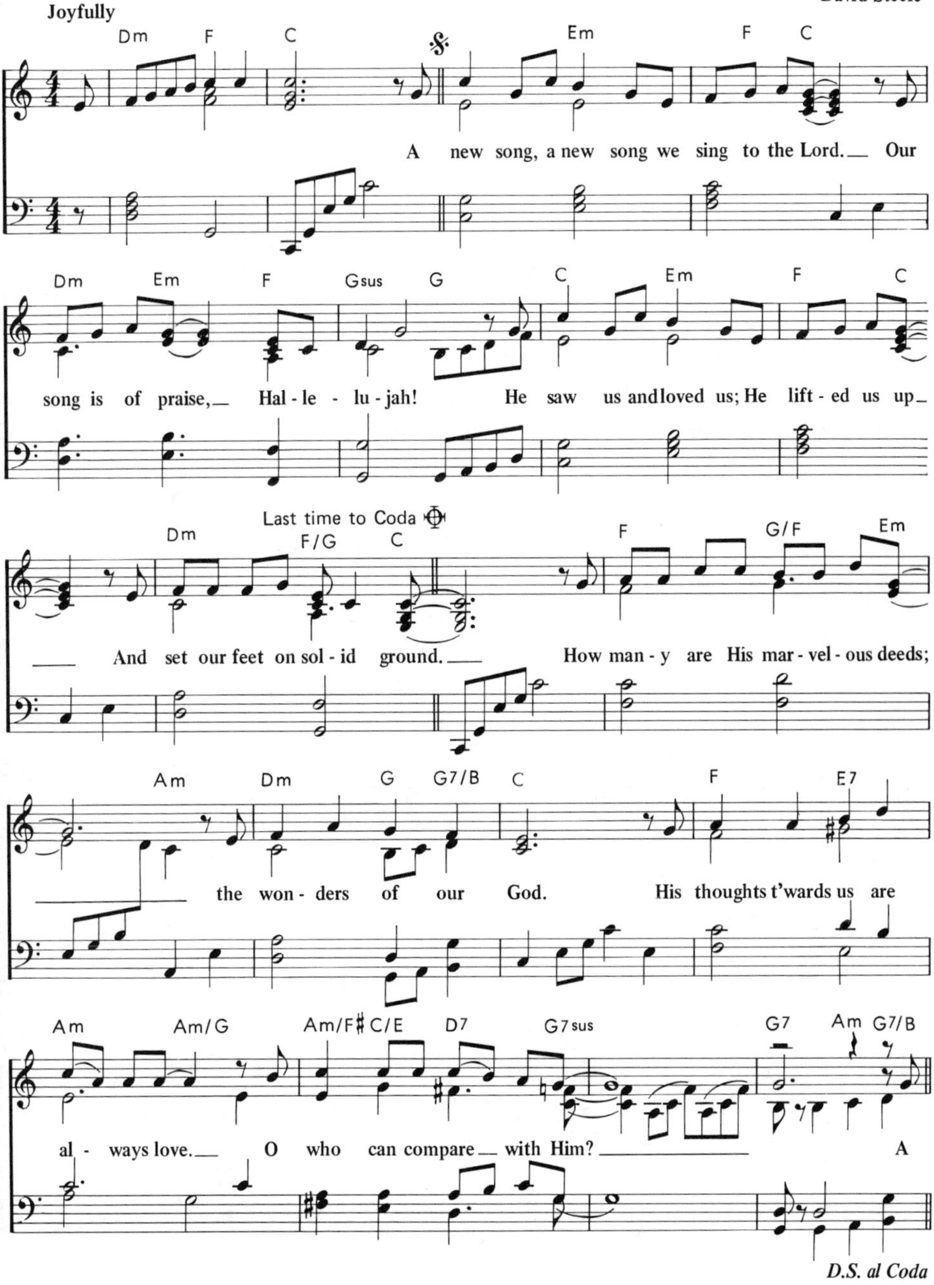
Joyfully
Dm F C Em F C
A new song, a new song we sing to the Lord. Our
Dm Em F Gsus G C Em F C
song is of praise, Hal-le-lu-jah! He saw us and loved us; He lift-ed us up
Last time to Coda
Dm F/G C F G/F Em
And set our feet on sol-id ground. How man-y are His mar-vel-ous deeds;
Am Dm G G7/B C F E7
the won-ders of our God. His thoughts t'wards us are
Am Am/G Am/F♯ C/E D7 G7sus G7 Am G7/B
al-ways love. O who can compare with Him? A
D.S. al Coda

Coda

Our song of praise we sing to God!

163
JESUS, PLEASE WATCH OVER US

Words and Music by
Robin Mann

With quiet dignity

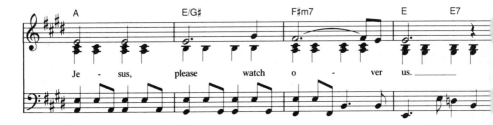

1. As we step from the edge of morn-ing, feet can't tell where to take us;
   Here's a light that will shine for - ev - er, Here's the light that will guide us.
2. Trou - ble comes, and we search for safe - ty, we for - get that you hold us;
   Fill our minds so that we re - mem-ber, Say once more that you love us.

Je - sus, please watch o - ver us. ___

Je - sus, please take care ___ of us.

3. Danger meets us at every moment,
   death is never in hiding;
   You are stronger than any danger,
   you are stronger than dying.

4. In your life is the Father's welcome,
   in your death there is freedom;
   Be our life and our death forever,
   Be our new resurrection.

PASS IT ON

Words & Music by
Kurt Kaiser

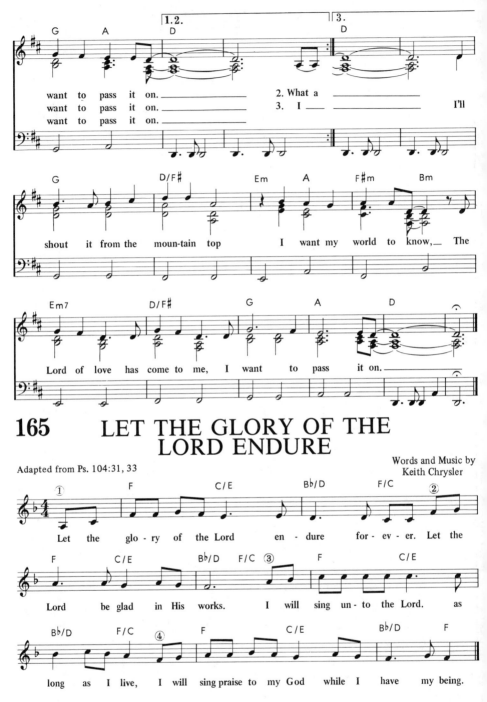

want to pass it on. _____
want to pass it on. _____   2. What a _____
want to pass it on. _____   3. I __ _____   I'll

shout it from the moun-tain top   I want my world to know,__ The

Lord of love has come to me,   I want to pass it on. _____

165   LET THE GLORY OF THE LORD ENDURE

Adapted from Ps. 104:31, 33

Words and Music by
Keith Chrysler

Let the glo-ry of the Lord en - dure for-ev-er. Let the

Lord be glad in His works.   I will sing un-to the Lord. as

long as I live, I will sing praise to my God while I have my being.

May also be used as a round

PRAISE HIM

166

Words and Music by
Tom Elie

167 PRAISE HIM, PRAISE HIM

Anon.

Praise Him, praise Him, all ye lit - tle chil - dren;
God is love, God is love.
Praise Him, praise Him, all ye lit - tle chil - dren;
God is love, God is love.

2. Love Him, 3. Thank Him, 4. Serve Him, 5. Crown Him,

PRAISE THE LORD

168

Words by
Chuck Girard, Jay Truax
and Herb Brendlin

Music by
Tom Coomes and Fred Field

1. Praise the Lord. Praise the Lord. Praise to Je - sus Christ from whom all bless-ings flow. Praise the Lord. Praise the Lord. Praise to Je - sus Christ from whom all bless-ings flow.

2. Praise His name. Praise His name. Praise His name and you will nev - er be the same. Praise His name. Praise His name. Praise His name and you will nev - er be the same.

Let's o - pen up our hearts. _____ Let the liv - ing wa - ter give our lives a start. Let's o - pen up our hearts. Let the liv - ing wa - ter give our lives a start.

169 PRAISE THE LORD

Words and Music by
Brown Bannister
Mike Hudson

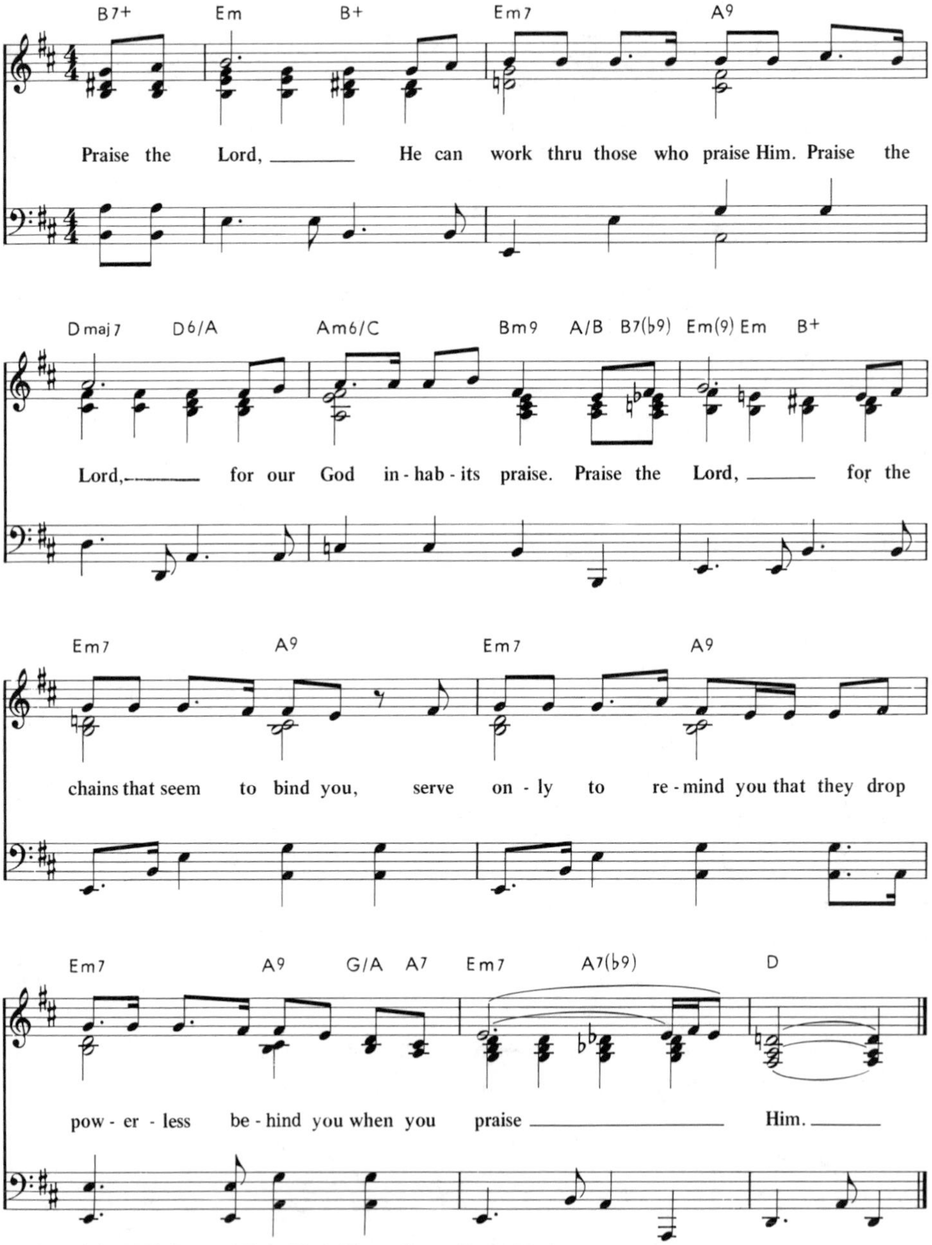

B7+ Em B+ Em7 A9
Praise the Lord, He can work thru those who praise Him. Praise the
Dmaj7 D6/A Am6/C Bm9 A/B B7(♭9) Em(9) Em B+
Lord, for our God in-hab-its praise. Praise the Lord, for the
Em7 A9 Em7 A9
chains that seem to bind you, serve on-ly to re-mind you that they drop
Em7 A9 G/A A7 Em7 A7(♭9) D
pow-er-less be-hind you when you praise Him.

PRAISE TO THE FATHER 170

Elizabeth Charles

Friedrich F. Flemming, 1778-1813

1. Praise to the Father for His lov - ing
2. Praise to the Sav - ior, great is His com -
3. Praise to the Spir - it, Com - fort - er of

kind - ness: Ten - der - ly cares He for His er - ring
pas - sion; Gra - cious - ly cares He for His chos - en
Is - rael, Sent of the Fa - ther and the Son to

chil - dren; Praise Him, all an - gels, praise Him in the
peo - ple; Young men and wom - en, ag - ing folk and
bless us, Praise to the Fa - ther, Son, and Ho - ly

heav - ens, Praise to Je - ho - vah.
chil - dren, Praise to the Sav - ior.
Spir - it, Praise to the Tri - une God.

171 PRAISE YOU, FATHER

Words and Music by
Jim Stipech

Praise ____ you, Fa - ther, ____ bless ____ you, Je - sus. ____

Ho - ly Spir - it, thank you for be - ing here, ____ be - ing here. ____

Praise ____ you, Fa - ther, ____ bless ____ you, Je - sus, ____ Ho - ly Spir - it,

thank you for be - ing here, ____ be - ing here ____ Lord. ____

PRAISE TO THE LORD 172

Joachim Neander
Tr. Catherine Winkworth

Stralsund Gesangbuch, 1665

1. Praise to the Lord, the Al - might - y, the King of cre - a - tion; O my soul, praise him, for he is thy health and sal - va - tion; All ye who hear, Now to his tem - ple draw near, Join - ing in glad ad - o - ra - tion.

2. Praise to the Lord, who o'er all things so won - drous - ly reign - eth, Shel - ters thee un - der his wings, yea, so gent - ly sus - tain - eth: Hast thou not seen How thy de - sires have been Grant - ed in what he or - dain - eth?

3. Praise to the Lord, who doth pros - per thy work and de - fend thee; Sure - ly his good - ness and mer - cy here dai - ly at - tend thee: Pon - der a - new What the Al - might - y can do, Who with his love doth be - friend thee.

4. Praise to the Lord! O let all that is in me a - dore him! All that hath life and breath, come now with prais - es be - fore him! Let the a - men Sound from his peo - ple a - gain: Glad - ly for ev - er a - dore him.

173 PRAISE THE NAME OF JESUS

Words and Music by
Roy Hicks

PRAYER OF ST. FRANCIS 174

Adapted by
Sebastian Temple

Music by Sebastian Temple
Arranged by Betty Carr Pulkingham

1. Make me a chan-nel of Your peace. _____ Where
2. Make me a chan-nel of Your peace. _____ Where
3. Make me a chan-nel of Your peace. _____ It

there is ha-tred, let me bring Your love. _____ Where
there's des-pair in life, let me bring hope. _____ Where
is in par-don-ing that we are par-doned, _____ in

there is in-ju-ry, Your par-don, Lord, _____ And
there is dark-ness — on-ly light, _____ And
giv-ing to all men that we re-ceive, _____

where there's doubt, true faith in You. _____
where there's sad-ness ev-er
dying that we're born to eternal life. _____

3rd time to Coda

joy. _____ Oh, Mas - ter, grant that I may nev - er

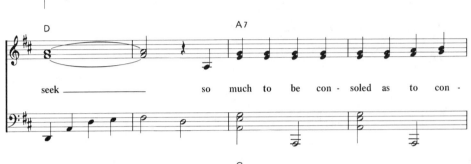

seek _____ so much to be con - soled as to con -

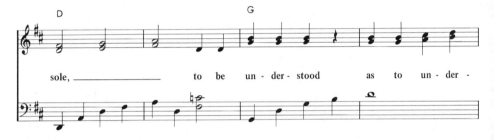

sole, _____ to be un - der - stood as to un - der -

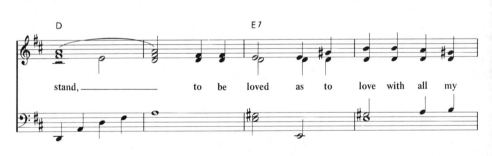

stand, _____ to be loved as to love with all my

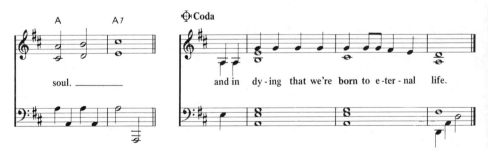

soul. _____ and in dy - ing that we're born to e -ter - nal life.

PSALM 8

175

Ewald Bash

Traditional American melody

1. O___ Lord, ___ our Lord, how ma - jes - tic your name is! How
2. When I think of the heav - ens, the work of your fin - gers, The
3. You___ made him, Lord in your own im - age and like - ness, And

great is your name___ in all ___ the earth!___ Your
moon and the stars you have set far in space, ___ What is
crowned him with hon - or and glo - ry; ___ You __

glo - ry is chant - ed a - bove the high heav - ens, You
man in your mem - 'ry a man that you're mind - ful, The
gave him do - min - ion o'er all of the wide earth, And

still all your foes through a child in his birth. ___
son ___ of man that you're car - ing for him. ___
o - ver the crea - tures that pass through the sea. ___

repeat stanza 1

176 RAISED FROM DEATH TO LOVE AND LIVING

Paul Sweetwater

1. Raised from death to love and living,
   Freed from sin to serve our Lord;
   Called to share His holy purpose,
   Know His likeness here restored;

2. What a loving, faithful father,
   Mighty God; who knows each need.
   All His paths are truth and kindness.
   When we daily let Him lead.

3. God, who knows our thoughts and actions,
   Soon will judge us by His Son.
   Each will then appear before Him,
   See His perfect justice done.

4. God, who planned and gave and suffered,
   Took our pain and death and sin.
   What a price to buy a sinner,
   Where can gratitude begin?

177 REST IN HIS LOVE AND ABIDE

Based on Romans 15:13
Paul Johnson

Bob Krogstad

May the God of hope touch you with His love As you
place your trust in His Son; May His gen - tle
Spir-it fill you with His joy As you walk by faith in what He's
done. May His peace fol - low you in be - liev - ing
As you find sweet re - lease in re - ceiv - ing;

178   COME, HOLY SPIRIT

J.W.P.

John W. Peterson
Arr. by Henry Wiens

1. The Ho-ly Spir-it came at Pen-te-cost, He came in might-y full-ness
2. Then in an age when dark-ness gripped the earth, "The just shall live by faith" was

then;____ His wit-ness thru be-liev-ers won the lost, And mul-ti-tudes were born a-
learned;__ The Ho-ly Spir-it gave the Church new birth As ref-or-ma-tion fires_

gain. The ear-ly Chris-tians scat-tered o'er the world,
burned. In la-ter years the great re-viv-als came,

They preached the gos-pel fear-less-ly;____ Tho some were mar-tyred and to
When saints would seek the Lord and pray;____ O once a-gain we need that

li-ons hurled, They marched a-long in vic-to-ry!
ho-ly Flame To meet the chall-enge of to-day!

179 ROAD IN WINTER

Words and Music by
Reynolds W. Guyer
Arr. by Henry Wiens

The road in win-ter_ is bit-ter and win-dy, Two lone-ly peo-ple_ are

tra-velled and worn; At last come to rest in a cold dus-ty sta-ble,

There___ a child___ is born; There a child___ is born.

1. Here comes the sun climb-in' bright on the hill-side, sounds in the town call-in'
2. said___ a child would be born in the win-ter, Enter in si-lence make
3. Here comes the sun climb-in' bright on the hill-side, sounds in the town call-in'

out the new day;___ Clear from a sta-ble the cry of a ba-by; Be-
read-y His way; His moth-er is gen-tle, His fa-ther is quiet; Be-
out the new day;___ Clear from a sta-ble the cry of a ba-by; Be-

180 REJOICE IN THE LORD ALWAYS

Philippians 4:4
Two Part Round

Words and Music by
Evelyn Tarner

Re - joice in the Lord — al - ways and a - gain I say re - joice re -

joice in the Lord — al - ways and a - gain I say re - joice Re -

joice re - joice and a - gain I say re - joice re -

joice re - joice and a - gain I say re - joice.

ROCK OF AGES, CLEFT FOR ME

181

August M. Toplady

Thomas Hastings

1. Rock of A - ges, cleft for me, Let me hide my - self in Thee; Let the wa - ter and the blood, From Thy riv - en side which flowed, Be of sin the doub - le cure, Save me from its guilt and pow'r.

2. Not the la - bor of my hands Can ful - fil Thy law's de - mands; Could my zeal no res - pite know, Could my tears for - ev - er flow, All for sin could not a - tone; Thou must save, and Thou a - lone.

3. Noth - ing in my hands I bring, Sim - ply to Thy cross I cling; Nak - ed, come to Thee for dress, Help - less look to Thee for grace; Foul, I to the foun - tain fly, Wash me. Sav - ior, or I die.

4. While I draw this fleet - ing breath, When my eyes shall close in death, When I soar to worlds un - known, See Thee on Thy judg - ment - throne, Rock of A - ges, cleft for me, Let me hide my - self in Thee.

182   PROMISES

Words and Music by
Terry K. Dittmer
Arr. by Henry Wiens

1. God said "That's e-nough, God said "That's e-nough, Of a world of sin and stuff!" Of a
2. Je-sus Christ was born, Je-sus Christ was born, One ear-ly Christ-mas morn, One
3. Prom-i-ses of love Prom-i-ses of love, Prom-i-ses of grace

world of sin and stuff!" So He sent a flood and then, So He sent a flood and then, The world could
ear-ly Christ-mas morn, And He died up-on a tree, And He died up-on a tree, He died for
Prom-i-ses of grace, Prom-i-ses of hope, Prom-i-ses of hope, Will put a

all start fresh a-gain, The world could all start fresh a-gain. Then He placed a rain-bow arc, Then He
you, He died for me, He died for you, He died for me. And we know that we are saved, And we
smile up-on your face, Will put a smile up-on your face. Prom-i-ses that bless,

placed a rain-bow arc, In the sky high o-ver-head, In the sky high o-ver-head, "And there'a
know that we are saved, 'Cause He rose up from the grave, 'Cause He rose up from the grave, And we
Prom-i-ses that bless, And prom-i-ses of joy, And prom-i-ses of joy,

nev - er be a flood, "And there'd nev - er be a flood, *Like that one back then," He said.* "Like that
know we're go'in to heav'n, And we know we're go'in to heav'n *That's a prom-ise we've been giv'n.* That's a
Prom - i - ses of God, Prom - i - ses of God, *Made to ev - ery girl and boy.* Made to

Chorus:

one back then," He said.
prom-ise we've been giv'n. Prom - i - ses, The Word of God is true, ___ Prom, - i - ses, They're
ev - ery girl and boy.

true for me and you, ___ Prom - i - ses, A guar-an-tee of love, ___ Prom - i - ses, A

gift from God a - bove, ___ Prom-i-ses, God's won-der-ful and great, ___ Prom-i-ses, We shout and cel-e-

brate, ___ Prom-i-ses, ___ Sing Al-le-lu! Al-le-lu - ia! ___

183 SAVIOR, LIKE A SHEPHERD LEAD US

Anonymous

William T. Bradbury

1. Sav - ior, like a shep-herd lead us, Much we need Thy ten - der care;
2. We are Thine, do Thou be - friend us, Be the Guar-dian of our way;
3. Thou hast prom-ised to re - ceive us, Poor and sin - ful though we be;
4. Ear - ly let us seek Thy fa - vor, Ear - ly let us do Thy will;

In Thy pleas -ant pas -tures feed us, For our use Thy folds pre - pare:
Keep Thy flock, from sin de - fend us, Seek us when we go a - stray;
Thou hast mer - cy to re - lieve us, Grace to cleanse, and pow'r to free:
Bless - ed Lord and on - ly Sav - ior, With Thy love our bos -oms fill:

Bless - ed Je - sus, Bless - ed Je - sus, Thou hast bought us, Thine we are;
Bless - ed Je - sus, Bless - ed Je - sus, Hear Thy chil - dren when they pray;
Bless - ed Je - sus, Bless - ed Je - sus, Ear - ly let us turn to Thee;
Bless - ed Je - sus, Bless - ed Je - sus, Thou hast loved us, love us still;

Bless - ed Je - sus, Bless - ed Je - sus, Thou hast bought us, Thine we are.
Bless - ed Je - sus, Bless - ed Je - sus, Hear Thy chil - dren when they pray.
Bless - ed Je - sus, Bless - ed Je - sus, Ear - ly let us turn to Thee.
Bless - ed Je - sus, Bless - ed Je - sus, Thou hast loved us, love us still.

* or A♭6

SHEPHERD OF LOVE 184

Words and Music by
John W. Peterson

C · C#° · Dm · Dm7 · G7 · C

Shep - herd of love,—— You knew I had lost my way; ——
Shep - herd of love, —— { Sav - ior and Lord and Guide, ——

C#° · Dm · Dm7 · G7 · 1. To next Score · C · C7

Shep - herd of of love, —— You cared that I'd gone— a - stray. ——
Shep - herd of of love, —— For - ev - er I'll stay by your

2. C · F · F#° · C · A7

side. ——— You sought and found me, placed a - round me

Fine

Dm · G7 · C · C7 · F · F#°

Strong arms that car - ried me home;—— No foe can harm me

C · A7 · Dm · D7 · G · G7

or a - larm me— Nev - er a - gain will I roam!——

D.C.

185 SOMETHING BEAUTIFUL

Gloria Gaither

William J. Gaither

Some - thing beau - ti - ful, some - thing good;

All my con - fu - sion___ He un - der - stood.

All I had to of - fer Him was bro - ken - ness and

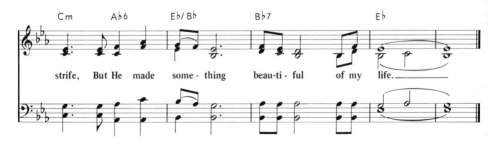

strife, But He made some - thing beau-ti - ful of my life.___

SING HALLELUJAH
(TO THE LORD)

186

Based on I Cor. 15:20, Rev.19:1

Linda Stassen

Additional verses
2. Jesus is risen from the dead.
3. Christ is the Lord of Heav'n and earth.
4. Praise be to God forevermore
5. Sing hallelujah to the Lord.

187 SEEK YE FIRST

Matt. 6:33

Karen Lafferty

Descant optional

1. Seek ye — first the — King-dom of God, And His — right - eous - ness.
2. Ask and — it shall be given un - to you, Seek and ye shall find,
3. Man does not live by bread a — lone, But by ev - ery word

And all these things shall be ad - ded un-to you! Al - le - lu, al-le - lu - ia!
Knock and the door shall be op - ened un-to you, Al - le - lu, al -le - lu - ia!
That pro — ceeds from the mouth of the Lord, Al - le - lu, al-le - lu - ia!

Vs. 2 and 3 not part of song as originally written.

SOMETIMES ALLELUIA 188

Words and Music by
Chuck Girard

Chorus

Some-times, "Al - le - lu - ia," some-times, "Praise the Lord,"___
Some-times gen - tly sing - ing, Our hearts in one ac - cord.___

Fine

Verse

1. Oh let us lift our voic - es,
2. Oh let us feel His pres - ence,
3. Oh let our joy be un - con - fined,
4. Oh let the Spir - it o - ver - flow,

Look to - ward the sky and start to sing;___
Let the sound of prais - es fill the air;___
Let us sing with free - dom un - re - strained;___
As ___ we are filled from head to toe.___

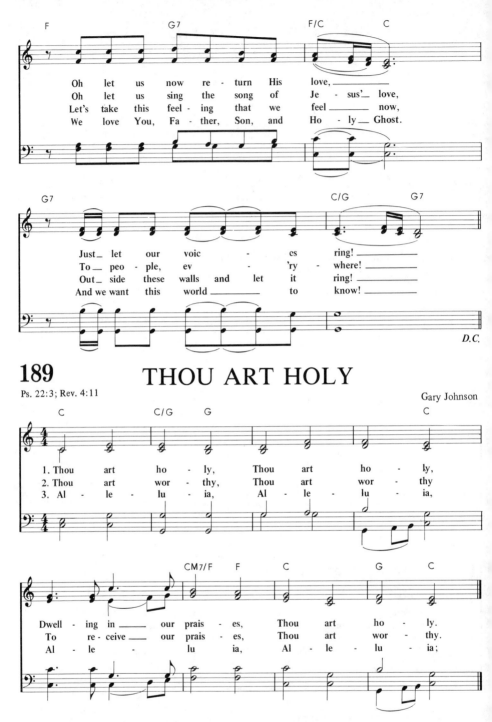

189 **THOU ART HOLY**

Ps. 22:3; Rev. 4:11

Gary Johnson

Verse lyrics:

1. Oh let us now re-turn His love, Just let our voic - es ring!
2. Oh let us sing the song of Je - sus' love, To peo - ple, ev - 'ry - where!
3. Let's take this feel - ing that we feel now, Out - side these walls and let it ring!
4. We love You, Fa - ther, Son, and Ho - ly Ghost. And we want this world to know!

D.C.

1. Thou art ho - ly, Thou art ho - ly, Dwell - ing in our prais - es, Thou art ho - ly.
2. Thou art wor - thy, Thou art wor - thy To re - ceive our prais - es, Thou art wor - thy.
3. Al - le - lu - ia, Al - le - lu - ia, Al - le - lu - ia, Al - le - lu - ia;

THE APOSTLES CREED 190

David Siebels
Arr. by Henry Wiens

I be-lieve in God, the Fa-ther, Al-might-y, Ma-ker of heav-en and earth, _____ and in Je-sus Christ, His on-ly Son, our Lord, _ Who was con-ceived by the Ho-ly Spir-it. _____ I be-lieve He was born of the Vir-gin Mar-y; suf-fered un-der Pon-tius Pi-late. He was cru-ci-fied, _____ died and was bur-ied. He de-scend-ed in-to Hell; _____ on the third day He rose a-gain from the dead, _____ A-

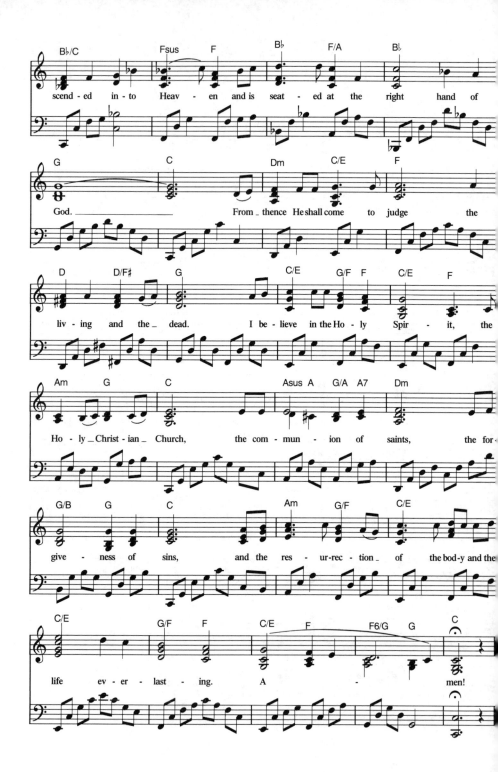

SOON AND VERY SOON   191

Words and Music by
Andrae Crouch

1. Soon and ver - y soon
2. No more cry - ing there,
3. No more dy - ing there,

we are going to see the King!

Soon and ver - y soon
No more cry - ing there,
No more dy - ing there,

we are going to see the King!

Soon and ver - y soon
No more cry - ing there,
No more dy - ing there,

we are

going to see the King!   Hal -le - lu - jah!   Hal -le - lu - jah!   We're

going to see the King!

going to see the King! ___

192 SOON THE DAY WILL COME

Words and Music by
John Worre

Soon the day will come when ev - 'ry knee shall bow,

Soon the day will come when ev - 'ry tongue shall con - fess _____ Je - sus is

Lord, _____ But I don't want to wait, I want to say it now.

I don't want to wait, so glad - ly I will con - fess: _____ Je - sus is

Lord, _____ Je - sus is Lord.

SPECIAL DELIVERY

193

Easily, with a lilt

Words and Music by
Ron and Carol Harris

SPIRIT OF GOD, DESCEND UPON MY HEART

194

George Croly

Frederick C. Atkinson

1. Spir - it of God, de - scend up on my heart;
2. Hast Thou not bid us love Thee, God and King?
3. Teach me to feel that Thou art al - ways nigh;
4. Teach me to love Thee as Thine an - gels love,

Wean it from earth through all its puls - es move;
All, all Thine own, soul, heart and strength and mind;
Teach me the strug - gles of the soul to bear,
One ho - ly pas - sion fill - ing all my frame;

Stoop to my weak - ness, might - y as Thou art,
I see Thy cross there teach my heart to cling:
To check the ris - ing doubt, the reb - el sigh;
The bap - tism of the heav'n de - scend - ed Dove,

And make me love Thee as I ought to love.
O let me seek Thee, and O let me find.
Teach me the pa - tience of un - an - swered prayer.
My heart an al - tar; and Thy love the flame. A - men.

195 SPIRIT OF THE LIVING GOD

Words and Music by
Daniel Iverson

SUCH AN OUT OF THE ORDINARY MAN

196

Words and Music by
John Worre
Arr. Henry Wiens

1. Some said He's just a man, an un-us-u-al man, But
2. hum-bly to John, tho' He was God's own Son, To
3. taught how to live, that you get what you give, To the

could He be more, E-ven part of God's plan? He seems dif-f'rent to me, It's not
be an ex-am-ple to all of His own, said a voice from a-bove "This is my
lost He had come for to seek and to save, He made blind eyes to see, set the

hard to a-gree, He could be the One, the Mes-si-ah to be, when I
son whom I love," and God's Ho-ly Spir-it came down like a Dove, He was
cap-tive ones free, lit-tle chil-dren He said "Let them come un-to me," Such

look in His eyes so sad and so wise, The wrong in my life I can
bap-tized that day in the wa-ter that way, But some-thing more hap-pened that
love He would show, and where ev-er He'd go, From Him liv-ing ri-vers of

SURELY GOODNESS AND MERCY

197

Based on Psalm 23

Words and Music by
John W. Peterson and
Alfred B. Smith

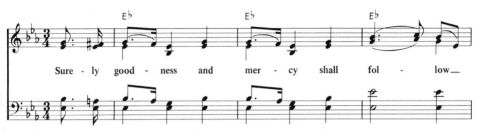

Sure - ly good - ness and mer - cy shall fol - low

me all the days, all the days of my life;

Sure - ly good - ness and mer - cy shall fol - low

me all the days, all the days of my life.

And I shall dwell in the house of the Lord for -

ev - er; And I shall feast at the ta - ble spread for me;

Sure - ly good - ness and mer - cy shall fol - low

me all the days, all the days of my life.

SWEET HOUR OF PRAYER 198

W. W. Walford

Wm. B. Bradbury

1. Sweet hour of prayer, sweet hour of prayer, That calls me from a world of care,
And bids me at my Fa - ther's throne Make all my wants and wish - es known,
In sea - sons of dis - tress and grief, My soul has oft - en found re - lief,
And oft es - caped the tempter's snare, By thy re - turn, sweet hour of prayer.

2. Sweet hour of prayer, sweet hour of prayer, Thy wings shall my pe - ti - tion bear,
To Him whose truth and faith - ful - ness En - gage the wait - ing soul to bless;
And since He bids me seek His face, Be - lieve His word and trust His grace,
I'll cast on Him my ev - 'ry care, And wait, for thee, sweet hour of prayer.

3. Sweet hour of prayer, sweet hour of prayer, May I thy con - so - la - tion share,
Till, from Mount Pisg - ah's loft - y height, I view my home, and take my flight:
This robe of flesh I'll drop, and rise To seize the ev - er - last - ing prize;
And shout, while pass - ing thro' the air, Fare - well, fare-well, sweet hour of prayer!

199
TAKE MY LIFE,
AND LET IT BE

Frances R. Havergal

C.H.A. Malan

1. Take my life, __ and __ let it be Con - se -
2. Take my feet, __ and __ let them be Swift and
3. Take my will, __ and __ make it Thine, It shall

cra - ted, __ Lord, to __ Thee; Take my hands, and __
beau - ti - ful for __ Thee; Take my voice, and __
be __ no __ long - er __ mine; Take my heart, it __

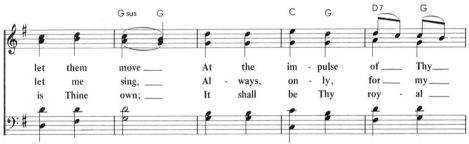

let them move __ At the im - pulse of __ Thy __
let me sing, __ Al - ways, on - ly, for __ my __
is Thine own; __ It shall be Thy roy - al __

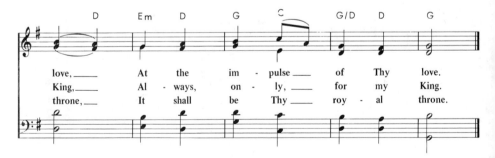

love, __ At the im - pulse __ of Thy love.
King, __ Al - ways, on - ly, __ for my King.
throne, __ It shall be Thy __ roy - al throne.

TELL THEM

200

Words and Music by
Andrae Crouch
Arr. Henry Wiens

Tell them ev-en if they don't be-lieve. You just tell them ev-en
Tell them when it seems you are for-sak-en, Just tell them tho' it

if they don't re-ceive, You just tell them for me. Please tell them for me — that I
seems your earth is shak-en, Just tell them for me. Please tell them for me — that I

love them, _____ And I came to let them know.
love them, _____ And I came to let them know.

Tell that lone-ly man — who walks the

cold streets all — a-lone. — Tell that cry-ing child who has no home.

THE BUILDING BLOCK 201

Words and Music by
Noel Paul Stookey

2. There is a man, there is a man, who has collected,
   all the sorrows in our eyes.
   He gives us love, as God directed,
   but is seldom recognized.
   CHORUS

3. When all your dreams, when all your dreams,
   have been connected,
   and your vision has been returned.
   Remember, love, you are protected,
   by the truth your heart has learned.
   CHORUS

202

THE CHURCH'S
ONE FOUNDATION

Samuel. J. Stone

Samuel S. Wesley

1. The Church-'s one foun-da-tion, Is Je-sus Christ her Lord;
2. E-lect from ev-'ry na-tion, Yet one o'er all the earth,
3. 'Mid toil and trib-u-la-tion, And tu-mult of her war,
4. Yet she on earth hath un-ion With God the Three in One,

She is His new cre-a-tion By wa-ter and the word:
Her char-ter of sal-va-tion' One Lord, one faith one birth;
She waits the con-sum-ma-tion Of peace for-ev-er-more;
And mys-tic sweet com-mun-ion With those whose rest is won:

From Heav'n He came and sought her To be His ho-ly bride; With
One ho-ly name she bless-es, Par-takes one ho-ly food, And
Till, with the vi-sion glo-rious, Her long-ing eyes are blest, And
O hap-py ones and ho-ly! Lord, give us grace that we, Like

His own blood He bought her, And for her life He died.
to one hope she press-es, With ev-'ry grace en-dued.
the great church vic-to-rious Shall be the church at rest.
them, the meek and low-ly, On high may dwell with Thee. A-men.

THE FAMILY OF GOD
203

William J. & Gloria Gaither

William J. Gaither

204 THE GREATEST THING

Words and Music by
Mark Pendergrass

THE JOY OF THE LORD 205

A G. V., alt.

Alliene G. Vale

206 THE KING OF GLORY

Willard F. Jabusch
Based on Ps. 24:7-10; Matt. 4:23-25; 9:33; I Pet. 3:18

Israeli Folk Song

Refrain

The King of glo - ry comes, the na - tion re - joic - es;

O - pen the gates be - fore Him, lift up your voic - es.

Fine

Stanzas

1. Who is the King of glo - ry; how shall we call Him?
2. In all of Gal - i - lee in cit - y or vil - lage,
3. Sing then of Da - vid's Son, our Sav - ior and Broth - er;
4. He gave His life for us, the Lamb of sal - va - tion;
5. He con - quered sin and death, He tru - ly has ris - en;

He is Em - man - u - el, the Prom - ised of a - ges.
He goes a - mong His peo - ple cur - ing their ill - ness.
In all of Gal - i - lee was nev - er an - oth - er.
He took up - on him - self the sins of the na - tion.
And He will share with us His heav - en - ly vi - sion.

D.C. al Fine

THE HIDING PLACE

207

Bryan Jeffery Leech

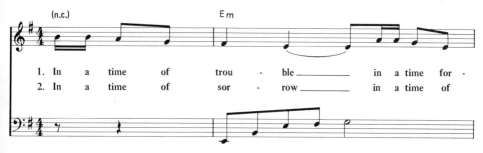

1. In a time of trou - ble _____ in a time for -
2. In a time of sor - row _____ in a time of

lorn, _____ There is a hid - ing place _____ where hope is
grief, _____ There is a hid - ing place _____ to give re -

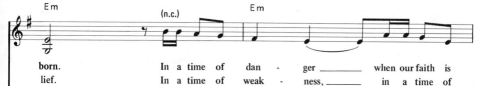

born. In a time of dan - ger _____ when our faith is
lief. In a time of weak - ness, _____ in a time of

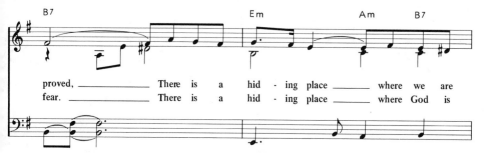

proved, _____ There is a hid - ing place _____ where we are
fear. _____ There is a hid - ing place _____ where God is

THE LAW OF THE LORD   208

Psalm 19:7-11,14

Jo Anne Roberts Graham

1. The law of __ the Lord is per-fect, ____ con-vert-ing __ the soul. __ The tes-ti-mon-y of the Lord is sure, ____ mak-ing wise the sim-ple. ____

Chorus
More to be de-sired are they than gold, yea, than much fine gold. __ Sweet-er al-so than hon-ey __ and the hon-ey-comb. ____

2. The statutes of the Lord are right,
   rejoicing the heart;
   The commandment of the Lord is pure.
   enlightening the eyes.

   Chorus

4. Let the words of my mouth, Oh Lord,   **Last**
   and the meditations of my heart,   **Chorus**
   Be acceptable in Thy sight, Oh Lord,
   my strength and my Redeemer.

3. The fear of the Lord is clean.
   enduring forever;
   The judgements of the Lord are true
   and righteous altogether.

   Chorus

   Moreover by them is Thy servant warned.
   is Thy servant warned.
   and in keeping of them there is great
   reward.

209 THE LORD BLESS THEE

Chuck Butler

THE LORD BLESS YOU
AND KEEP YOU

Farewell Anthem With Sevenfold Amen

Words and Music by
Peter C. Lutkn

210

The Lord bless you and keep. you, the Lord lift His coun - te-nance up -

on you; and give you peace, and give you, peace, and give you peace, and give you peace, the Lord, the

Lord make His face to shine up - on you, and be and be gracious

and be gra - cious, the Lord be gra-cious, gra - cious un - to

you. A - men, A - men, A - men A - men A - men

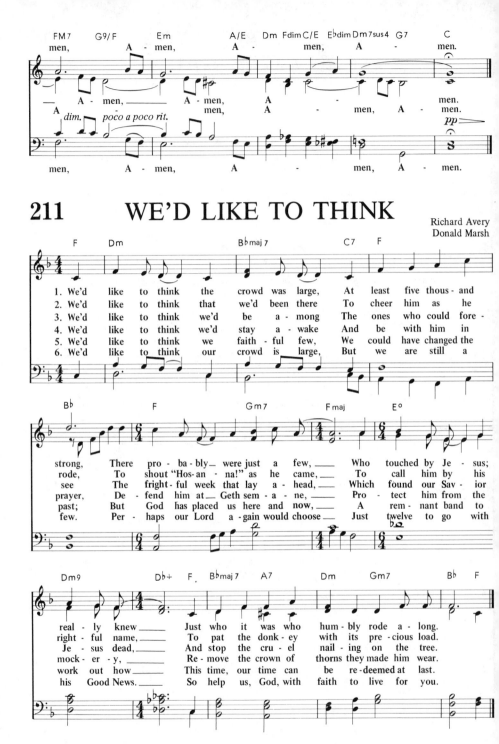

211   WE'D LIKE TO THINK

Richard Avery
Donald Marsh

1. We'd like to think the crowd was large, At least five thous-and
2. We'd like to think that we'd been there To cheer him as he
3. We'd like to think we'd be a - mong The ones who could fore -
4. We'd like to think we'd stay a - wake And be with him in
5. We'd like to think we faith - ful few, We could have changed the
6. We'd like to think our crowd is large, But we are still a

strong, There pro - ba - bly— were just a few, ___ Who touched by Je - sus;
rode, To shout "Hos-an - na!" as he came, ___ To call him by his
see The fright - ful week that lay a - head, ___ Which found our Sav - ior
prayer, De - fend him at— Geth sem - a - ne, ___ Pro - tect him from the
past; But God has placed us here and now, ___ A rem - nant band to
few. Per - haps our Lord a - gain would choose — Just twelve to go with

real - ly knew ___ Just who it was who hum - bly rode a - long.
right - ful name, ___ To pat the donk - ey with its pre - cious load.
Je - sus dead, ___ And stop the cru - el nail - ing on the tree.
mock - er - y, ___ Re - move the crown of thorns they made him wear.
work out how ___ This time, our time can be re - deemed at last.
his Good News. ___ So help us, God, with faith to live for you.

THE LORD IS MY LIGHT 212

Ps. 27:1

Music by Paune M. Mills
Arr. by Charles High

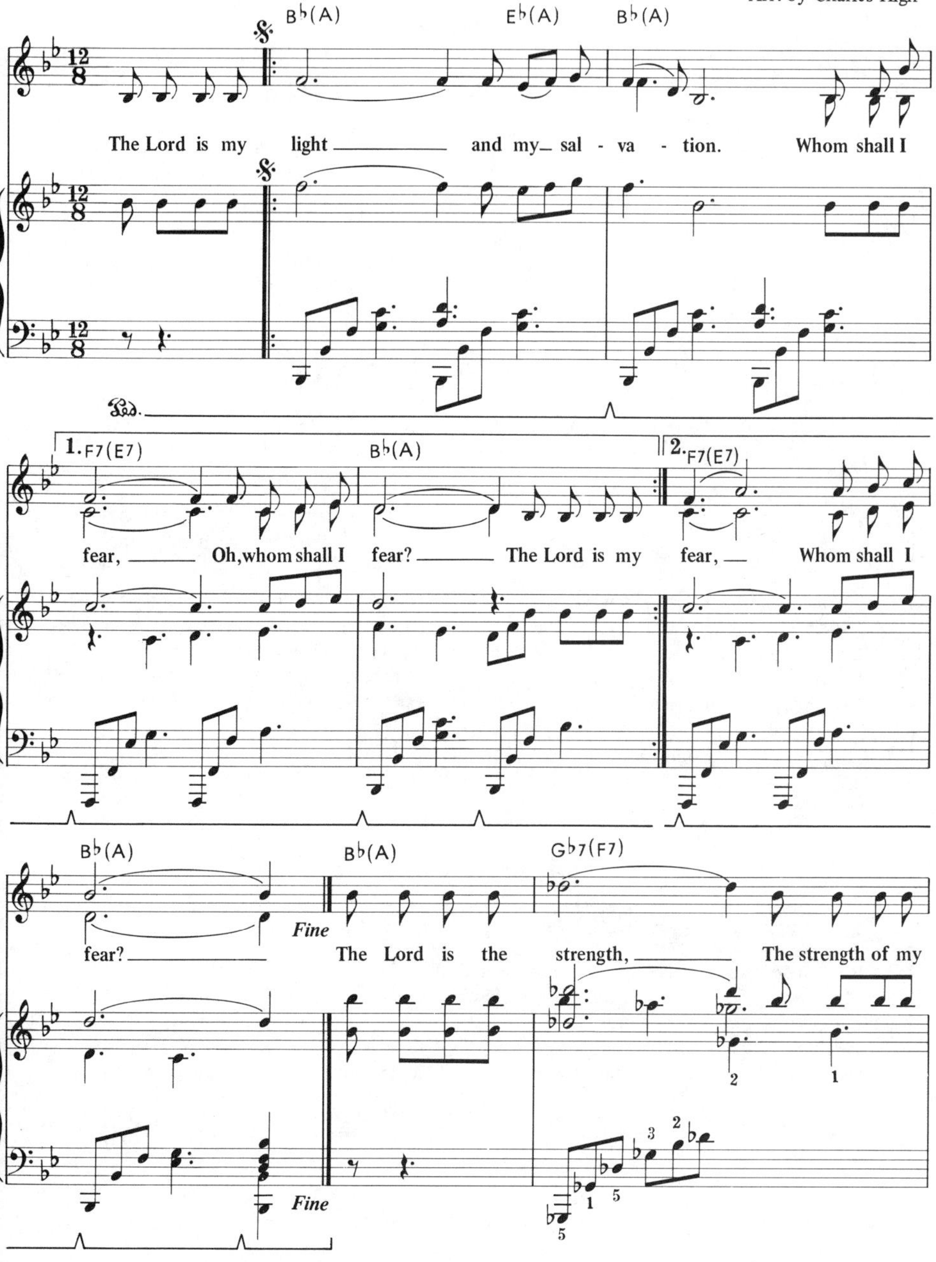

B♭(A) E♭(A) B♭(A)
The Lord is my light and my sal - va - tion. Whom shall I
1. F7(E7) B♭(A) 2. F7(E7)
fear, Oh, whom shall I fear? The Lord is my fear, Whom shall I
B♭(A) B♭(A) G♭7(F7)
fear? Fine The Lord is the strength, The strength of my
Fine

213
HALLELUJAH, WHAT A SAVIOUR!

Words and Music by
P. P. Bliss

THERE WERE TWELVE DISCIPLES
(HE HAS CALLED US TOO) 214

non.

George A. Minor

There were twelve dis-ci - ples Je - sus called to help him: Si - mon Pe - ter, An - drew,

James, his bro - ther John; Phil - ip, Thom - as, Mat - thew, James, the son of Al - pheus,

Chorus

Thad-deus, Si - mon, Ju - das, And Bar - thol - o-mew. He has called us too,

He has called us too; We are His dis-ci - ples, I am one and you. ples, We his work must do.

215 THE LORD IS MY SHEPHERD

Based on Psalm 23

With assurance

Unknown

The Lord is my___ shep - herd I'll live for Him al -

ways, He leads in green___ pas - tures, I'll live for Him al -

ways. Al - ways, al - ways, I'll live for Him al - ways. Al -

ways. al - ways, I'll live for Him al - ways. The ways.

THE LORD IS PRESENT IN HIS SANCTUARY

216

Words and Music by
Gail Cole

1. The Lord is pres-ent in His sanc - tu-ar - y, let us praise __ the Lord. The
2. The Lord is pres-ent in His sanc - tu-ar - y, let us delight in the Lord. The
3. The Lord is pres-ent in His sanc - tu-ar - y, let us serve __ the Lord. The

Lord is pres - ent in His sanc - tu-ar - y, let us praise __ the Lord.
Lord is pres - ent in His sanc - tu-ar - y, let us delight in the Lord.
Lord is pres - ent in His sanc - tu-ar - y, let us serve __ the Lord.

Praise Him, praise __ Him, __ let us praise __ the Lord. __

Praise Him, praise __ Him, __ let us praise __ Je - sus.

217 EVERY EYE SHALL SEE

Words by William J. and Gloria Gaither

Music by William J. Gaither
Arr. by Alex Galvan

THE LOVE ROUND 218

Three Part Round

Unknown
Arranged by Charles High

Love, love, love, love, Chris - tians, this is your__ call; Love your neigh - bor as your - self, for God loves us all. all.

219 THE NEW 23RD

Psalm 23
Adapted by R.C.

Ralph Carmichael

Be - cause the Lord is my shep - herd, I have ev - 'ry-thing that I need, He lets me rest in mead-ows green And leads me be-side the qui - et stream. He keeps on giv - ing life to me And helps me to do what hon - ors Him the most. E - ven when walk-ing thru the dark val - ley of death, val - ley of death, I will nev - er be a-fraid, for He is close be - side me. Guard-ing, guid-ing all the

220 THE OLD RUGGED CROSS

Words and Music by
George Bennard

1. On a hill far a-way stood an old rug-ged cross, The em-blem of suf-f'ring and shame; And I love that old cross where the dear-est and best For a world of lost sin-ners was slain.
2. O that old rug-ged cross, so de-spised by the world, Has a won-drous at-trac-tion for me; For the dear Lamb of God left His glo-ry a-bove To bear it to dark Cal-va-ry.
3. In the old rug-ged cross, stained with blood so di-vine, A won-drous beau-ty I see; For 'twas on that old cross Je-sus suf-fered and died To par-don and sanc-ti-fy me.
4. To the old rug-ged cross, I will ev-er be true, Its shame and re-proach glad-ly bear; Then He'll call me some day to my home far a-way, Where His glo-ry for-ev-er I'll share.

Chorus

So I'll cher-ish the old rug-ged cross, the old rug-ged cross, Till my

tro - phies at last I lay down; ____ I will cling to the old rug - ged
cross, the

cross, _____ And ex - change it some day for a crown. ____
old rug - ged cross,

THANK YOU, LORD

221

Words and Music by
Mr. and Mrs. Seth Sykes

Thank you, Lord, for sav - ing my soul. Thank you, Lord, for mak-ing me whole;

Thank you, Lord, for giv - ing to me Thy great sal - va - tion so rich and free.

222 THE SOLID ROCK

Edward Mote

William B. Bradbury

1. My hope is built on noth-ing less Than Je - sus blood and right-eous-ness;
2. When dark-ness seems to hide His face, I rest on His un - chang-ing grace;
3. His oath, His cov - e - nant, His blood, Sup - port me in the whelm-ing flood;
4. When He shall come with trum-pet sound, Oh, may I then in Him be found;

I dare not trust the sweet-est frame, But whol-ly lean on Je - sus' name.
In ev - er-y high and storm-y gale, My an-chor holds with - in the vale.
When all a - round my soul gives way, He then is all my hope and stay.
Dressed in His right - eous - ness a - lone, Fault - less to stand be - fore the throne.

Refrain

On Christ, the sol - id Rock, I stand: All oth - er ground is
sink - ing sand, All oth - er ground is sink - ing sand.

THERE'S A QUIET UNDERSTANDING

223

Words and Music by
Tedd Smith

1. There's a qui - et un - der - stand - ing when we're gath - ered in the Spir it; It's a prom - ise that He gives us, when we gath - er in His name. There's a love we feel in Je - sus, there's a man - na that He feeds us, It's a prom - ise that He gives us When we gath - er in His name.

2. And we know when we're to - geth - er, shar - ing love and un - der - stand - ing, That our broth - ers and our sis - ters feel the one - ness that He brings. Thank You, thank You, thank You, Je - sus, for the way You love and feed us, For the man - y ways You lead us, Thank You, thank You, Lord.

224 THE WISE MAN AND THE FOOLISH MAN

Matthew 7:24-27

Arr. by Harry Dixon Loes

1. The wise man built his house up-on the rock, The wise man built his
2. The fool-ish man built his house up-on the sand, The fool-ish man built his

house up-on the rock; The wise man built his house up-on the rock,
house up-on the sand; The fool-ish man built his house up-on the sand,

And the rains came tum-bling down.

Chorus

The rains came down and the floods came up, The rains came down and the floods came up; The

rains came down and the floods came up, And the house on the rock stood fast.
And the house on the sand went smash.

Add this Verse No. 3

So build your Life on the Lord Jesus Christ,
So build your Life on the Lord Jesus Christ,
So build your Life on the Lord Jesus Christ,
And the blessings will come down

Chorus 3 V. only

The blessings come down as the prayers go up,
The blessings come down as the prayers go up,
The blessings come down as the prayers go up,
So build your Life on the Lord.

I LOVE YOU, LORD 225

Words and Music by
Laurie Klein

226
THERE IS A FLAG
(JOY IS THE FLAG)

Words and Music by
Brian Konzelman

There is a flag flown from the cas-tle of my heart, The cas-tle of my heart, the cas-tle of my heart. There is a flag flown from the cas-tle of my heart when the King is in res-i-dence there. So raise it high in the sky, let the whole world know, let the whole world know, let the whole world know. So raise it high in the sky, let the

G#dim 7   D/A   A7   D

whole world know that the King is in res - i - dence there.

JUST A CLOSER WALK
WITH THEE

227

Text adapted by N. J.

Traditional Spiritual

G Sing chorus first and after each stanza   D 7

| | | | | | | |
Chorus: Just | a | clos - er | walk | with | Thee ____ Grant | it | Je -
1. I | am | weak but | Thou | art | strong ____ Je - | sus, | keep
2. Thru | this | world of | toil | and | snares, ____ If | I | fal -
3. When | my | fee - ble | life | is | o'er, ____ Time | for | me

G   G 7

sus, | if | you - | please; ____ | Dai - | ly | walk - ing | close | to
me | from | all | wrong; ____ | I'll | be | sat - is - fied | as
ter, | Lord, | who | cares? ____ | Who | with | me my | bur - den
will | be | no | more; ____ | On | that | bright e - | ter - nal

C   G   D 7   G

Thee ____ | Let it | be, | dear Lord, | let it | be.
long ____ | As I | walk, | dear Lord, | close to | Thee.
shares? ____ | None but | Thee, | dear Lord, | none but | Thee.
shore ____ | I will | walk, | dear Lord, | close to | Thee.

228 JESUS, WE JUST WANT TO THANK YOU

Words and Music by
William J. Gaither
Arr. by Henry Wiens

Je - sus, we just want to [thank praise] you. _____ Je - sus, we just want to [thank praise] _____ you, Je - sus, we just want to [thank praise] You, _____ [thank Praise] You for be - ing so good. good. _____

HEAR, O LORD, I RAISE MY VOICE

229

Norman Habel

"Michael"

1. Hear O Lord, I raise my voice, Al - le - lu -
2. You're my shield, and guard me true Al - le - lu -
3. Shouts of glo - ry to the Father Al - le - lu -

ia! You're my help, and I re - joice, Al - le - lu -
ia! Lord of Hosts, You keep us now Al - le - lu -
ia! Shouts of glo - ry to His Son, Al - le - lu -

ia! The Lord's my lamp who lights my way, Al - le - lu -
ia! Hear O Lord, I raise my voice, Al - le - lu -
ia! Shouts of glo - ry to the Spirit, Al - le - lu -

ia. With His help. I can not stray, Al - le - lu - ia!
ia. You're my help. and I re - joice, Al - le - lu - ia!
ia. As it was! and has to be, Al - le - lu - ia!

4. Hear, O Lord, I raise my voice, Alleluia!
You're my help, and I rejoice, Alleluia.
The Lord's my lamp who lights my way, Alleluia.
With His help, I cannot stray, Alleluia!

Used by permission.

230 THERE'S NO GREATER NAME

Words and Music by
Michael Baughan

1. There's no great - er name than Je - sus,
   name of him who came to save us,
   In that sav - ing name of Je - sus
   Ev' - ry knee should bow.

2. In our minds by faith pro - fess - ing,
   In our hearts by in - ward bless - ing,
   On our tongues by words con -

231 THEREFORE THE REDEEMED

Isa. 51:11

Ruth Lake

Lyrics:

There - fore the re -deemed of the Lord shall re - turn. re - turn and come with sing - ing____ un - to Zi - on. ____ and ev - er - last - ing____ joy shall be up - on their heads. ____ There - fore the re - deemed of the Lord shall re - turn. re - turn __ and come with sing-ing _____ un - to Zi - on. ____ and ev - er - last - ing____ joy shall be up - on their

heads. _____ They shall ob - tain glad - ness and

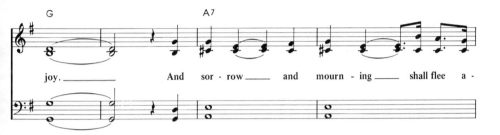

joy. _____ And sor - row ____ and mourn - ing ____ shall flee a -

way. _____ There - fore the re -deemed of the Lord shall re -

turn. re - turn_ and come with sing - ing_____ un - to Zi - on, _____ and ev - er-

last - ing__ joy shall be up - on their heads. _____

232

THEY THAT WAIT
UPON THE LORD

Adapted from Is. 40:31

Stuart Hamblen

THIS IS MY COMMANDMENT **233**

John 15:11-12

Arr. Betty Pulkingham

Simply

This is my command-ment that you love one an-oth-er, that your

joy may be full.

full: that your

joy_____ may be full,_____ that your

joy_____ may be full._____

Fine

D.C. al Fine

Other verses may be added:

eg. This is my commandment that you 'trust one another. . . '

'serve one another . . . '

'lay down your lives . . . '

234 THIS IS THE DAY

Psalm 118:24

Les Garrett

This is the day, this is the day that the Lord hath made, that the Lord hath made. I will re-joice, I will re-joice and be glad in it, and be glad in it, This is the day that the Lord hath made, we will re-joice and be glad in it. This is the day, this is the day that the Lord hath made.

THIS LITTLE LIGHT OF MINE 235

Arr. by Harry Dixon Loes

236 THOU ART WORTHY

Rev. 4:11

Pauline M. Mills

Thou art wor - thy, Thou art wor - thy,
Thou art wor - thy, O Lord, _____ To re - ceive
glo - ry, glo - ry and hon - or glo - ry and hon - or and
power. _____ For Thou hast cre - a - ted, hast all things cre -
a - ted; Thou hast cre - a - ted all things. _____

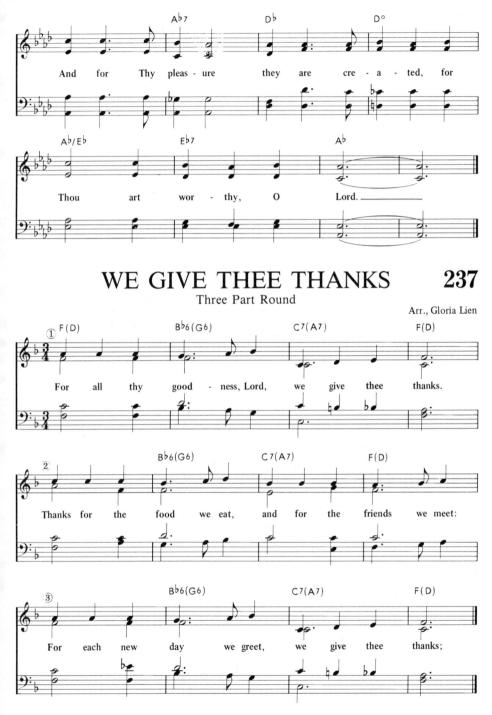

And for Thy pleas - ure they are cre - a - ted, for

Thou art wor - thy, O Lord.

WE GIVE THEE THANKS **237**
Three Part Round

Arr., Gloria Lien

For all thy good - ness, Lord, we give thee thanks.

Thanks for the food we eat, and for the friends we meet:

For each new day we greet, we give thee thanks;

238 THROUGH IT ALL

Words and Music by
Andraé Crouch

1. I've had man - y tears and sor - rows; I've had ques - tions for
2. I've been to lots of pla - ces, And I've seen a lot
3. I thank God for the moun-tains, And I thank Him for

to - mor - row; there've been times I did'n't know right from
of fa - ces, there've been times I felt so all a -
the val - leys, I thank him for the storms He brought me

wrong; But in ev - 'ry sit - u -
lone; But in my lone - ly
through For if I'd nev - er

a - tion God gave bless - ed con - so - la - tion that my
ho - urs, yes those pre - cious lone - ly ho - urs, Je - sus
had a prob - lem, I would - n't know that He could solve them, I'd

239 THY LOVING KINDNESS

Adapted from Ps. 63:3-4

Hugh Mitchell

1. Thy lov - ing kind - ness is bet - ter than life.
2. I lift my hands, Lord, un - to Thy name.

Thy lov - ing kind - ness is bet - ter than life.
I lift my hands, Lord, un - to Thy name.

My lips shall praise Thee, thus, will I bless Thee
My lips shall praise Thee, thus will I bless Thee

I will lift up my hands un - to Thy Name.
I will lift up my hands un - to Thy Name.

TURN YOUR EYES UPON JESUS 240

Words and Music by
Helen H. Lemmel

241 TO GOD BE THE GLORY

Fanny J. Crosby

William H. Doane

242 TWO HANDS

Words and Music by
Tom Coomes & Chuck Butler
Arr. Gloria Lien

1. We're all gath-ered here _____ Be-cause we all be-lieve.
2. Man-y know him well, _____ Oth-ers just by name.

If there's a doubt-er in the crowd, _____ We ask you
If you don't know for what he stands, _____ You've real-ly

not to leave;
much to gain;
Give a lis-ten to his
With _____ faith you can move

sto-ry;
moun-tains;
Hear the mes-sage that we bring.
These are com-mon words but true.

243 UNTO THEE O LORD

Psalm 25: 12,4

Charles Monroe

Un - to thee o Lord do I lift up — my soul ___ un - to thee o Lord

Do I lift up ___ my soul ___ o my God ___

I trust in thee Let me not be a - shamed.

Let not my en - e - mies triumph ___ ov - er me. ___

WE ARE FAMILY
244

Words and Music by
Jimmy and Carol Owens

1. We are heirs of the Fa - ther.
We are joint heirs with the Son.
We are chil - dren of the King - dom.
We are fam - i - ly. We are one.

2. We are washed, we are sanctified,
   We are cleansed by His blood,
   We are born of the Spirit,
   We are children of the Lord.

3. We are longing for His coming.
   We are looking to the skies,
   We are watching, we are waiting,
   We will fly with Him, we will rise.

4. We will reign with Him forever.
   Men and angels shout and sing,
   All dominion shall be given
   To the family of the King.

245 WE ARE THE CHURCH

Words and Music by
Richard Avery and Donald Marsh

1. The church is not a build - ing, The church is not a stee - ple, The church is not a rest - ing place, The church is a peo - ple!
2. We're man - y kinds of peo - ple, With man - y kinds of fac - es, All col - ors and all a - ges, too, From all times and plac - es.
3. Some - times the church is march - ing, Some - times it's brave - ly burn - ing, Some - times it's rid - ing, some - times hid - ing, Al - ways it's learn - ing:
4. And when the peo - ple gath - er There's sing - ing and there's pray - ing, There's laugh - ing and there's cry - ing some - times, All of it say - ing:
5. At Pen - te - cost some peo - ple Re - ceived the Ho - ly Spir - it And told the Good News thru the world to All who would hear it.
6. I count if I am nin - ty Or nine or just a ba - by; There's one thing I am sure a - bout and I don't mean may - be;

D.C.

WHAT A FRIEND

Joseph Scriven

Charles C. Converse

1. What a Friend we have in Je - sus, All our sins and griefs to bear!
2. Have we tri - als and temp - ta - tions, Is there trou- ble an - y - where?
3. Are we weak and heav - y - la - den, Cum - bered with a load of care?

What a priv - i - lege to car - ry Ev - ery-thing to God in prayer!
We should nev - er be dis - cour - aged, Take it to the Lord in prayer.
Pre - cious Sav - iour, still our ref - uge, Take it to the Lord in prayer.

O what peace we of - ten for - feit, O what need-less pain we bear,
Can we find a friend so faith - ful Who will all our sor-rows share?
Do thy friends de -spise, for- sake thee? Take it to the Lord in prayer;

All be - cause we do not car - ry Ev - ery -thing to God in prayer!
Je - sus knows our ev - ery weak - ness, Take it to the Lord in prayer.
In His arms He'll take and shield thee, Thou wilt find a sol -ace there.

247

WE ARE THE REASON

Words and Music by
David Meece

Slowly, with building intensity

We were the rea - son that He gave His life,__ we were the rea - son that He suf-fered and died.__ To a world that was lost,__ He gave all__ He could give,__ to show us the rea - son to live. live. I've fin 'lly found a rea-son for liv - ing, it's in giv - ing ev-'ry part of my heart.

248 WE WILL LIFT UP YOUR NAME

Based on Ps. 34:1-3

Glen Aubrey

2.

F/C C C#° Dm11 Dm7/F G/F

Lord. _____ No oth - er name we know that is

Em7 C9 Fm7

wor - thy of praise; No oth - er Sav - ior we

Ab/Bb Gm/Bb Fm/Bb B°/D C C7 F

wor - ship but Je - sus. Lamb of __ God, Prince of

G/F E7 Am11 Am

Peace, the might - y Con - queror is He; And we'll

D7 Dm7 G7

lift up His __ name for - ev - er. _____ We will

D.S. al Fine

249 WE HAVE COME INTO HIS HOUSE

Words and Music by
Bruce Ballinger

1. We have come in-to His house gath-ered in His name to wor - ship Him. We have come in-to His house gath-ered in His name to wor - ship Him. We have come in-to His house gath-ered in His name to wor - ship Christ the Lord, Wor - ship Him, Christ the Lord.

2. So let's lift up holy hands, and magnify His name, and worship Him . . .
3. So forget about yourself, and concentrate on Him, and worship Him . . .
4. He is all my righteousness, I stand complete in Him, and worship Him . . .

WHEN HE COMETH

Rev. W. O. Cushing

Geo. F. Root

1. When He com - eth, when He com - eth To make up His
2. He will gath - er, He will gath - er The gems for His
3. Lit - tle chil - dren, lit - tle chil - dren Who love their Re -

jew - els, All His jew - els, pre -cious jew - els, His loved and His own.
king - dom, All the pure ones, all the bright ones, His loved and His own.
deem - er, Are the jew - els, pre -cious jew - els, His loved and His own.

Chorus

Like the stars of the morn - ing,, His bright crown a - dorn - ing, They shall

shine in their beaut - y, Bright gems for His crown.

251 ZACCHAEUS

Unknown

Music arr. by
Mrs. N. R. SCHAPER

F C7 F C7 F C7
1 Zac - chae - us was a wee lit - tle man, 2 A wee lit - tle man was
F C7 F C7 F C7
he, 3 He climbed up in a sy - ca - more tree 4 For the Lord he want-ed to
F C7 F C7 F C7
see; And as the Sav - iour passed that way, 5 He looked up in the
F C7
tree, 6 Spoken And He said: "Zacchaeus, you come down, 7 For I'm go - ing to your house to -
F G7 C7 F
day, For I'm go - ing to your house to - day."

① Hands in front, right palm raised above left palm. ② Bring palms a little closer. ③ Alternate hands in climbing motion. ④ Shade eyes with right hand and look down. ⑤ Shade eyes with right hands and look up. ⑥ Words are spoken, while looking up and wagging a finger in admonition.
⑦ Clap hands on accented beat.

ZEPHANIAH 3:17

Tapu Moala

253   WE ARE FREE IN HIM

Source Unknown

1. We are free in Him; we are free in Him; and no one can take Him a way. We are
2. saved in Him; we are saved in Him; and no one can take Him a way. We are
3. Sav - ior; He's our Sav - ior and no one can take Him a way. He's our way.

He's our way. 2. We are 3. He's our way.

He is com - ing; He is com - ing and no one can keep Him a way.

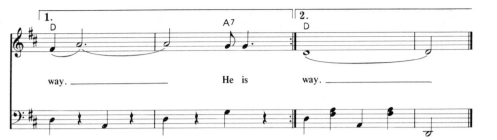

way. _____ He is way. _____

WHEN I REMEMBER 254

Source Unknown

Chorus:

No, no, no, no, no, _ I'll nev-er_ go back an-y-more, hal-le-lu-ia._

nev-er_ go back an-y-more. 1. When I re-mem-ber that he died for me,_ I'll

Verse:

nev-er_ go back an-y-more, hal-le-lu-ia._ nev-er_ go back an-y-more.

Chorus

2. When I remember that He rose again . . . .
   CHORUS

3. When I remember that He lives in me . . .
   CHORUS

4. When I remember that He's coming soon . . .
   CHORUS

255 WIND, WIND

Jane and Betsy Clowe

Jane Clowe

Wind, wind, blow on me;___ wind, wind, set me free;___

wind, wind, my Fa - ther sent the bless - ed Ho - ly Spi - rit.___

Last time

1. Je - sus told us all a - bout___ you,
2. When we're wea - ry you con - sole ___ us;
3. When un - to the Church you came,___ it was
4. Set us free to love our bro - thers;

how we could not live with - out___ you, with his blood - the
when we're lone - ly you en - fold___ us; when in dan - ger
not in your own but Je - sus' name. Je - sus Christ is
set us free to live for oth - ers that the world the

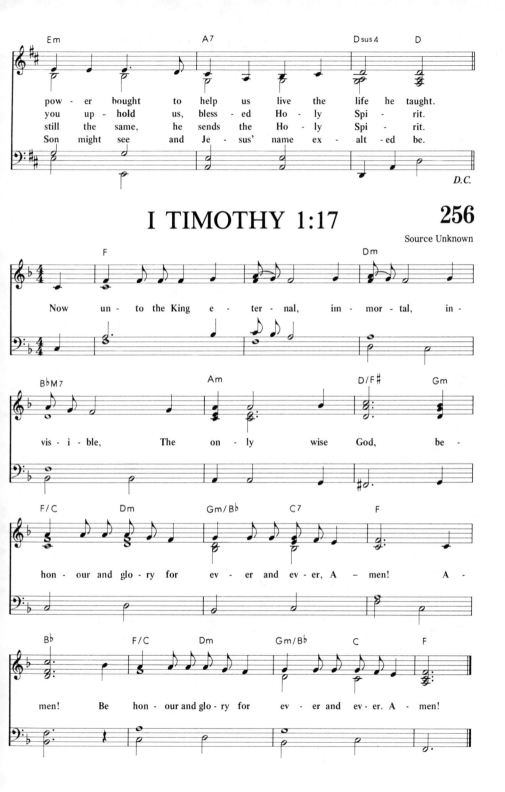

pow - er bought to help us live the life he taught.
you up - hold us, bless - ed Ho - ly Spi - rit.
still the same, he sends the Ho - ly Spi - rit.
Son might see and Je - sus' name ex - alt - ed be.

D.C.

I TIMOTHY 1:17

256

Source Unknown

Now un - to the King e - ter - nal, im - mor - tal, in -

vis - i - ble, The on - ly wise God, be -

hon - our and glo - ry for ev - er and ev - er, A - men! A -

men! Be hon - our and glo - ry for ev - er and ev - er. A - men!

257 WE ARE MADE IN THE IMAGE OF GOD

Words and Music by
Gloria Lien

1. We are made in the im-age of God — We're low-er than the an-gels We're His
2. We are made in the im-age of God — We're low-er than the an-gels We're His

num-ber one cre-a-tion made in the im-age of God We are
num-ber one cre-a-tion made in the im-age of God We are

made to have dominion over ev-'ry liv-ing thing made to en-joy the
one __ of a kind __ spe-cial and un-ique made for a purpose to

fruits of this land Made to love God Made to love each oth er
Glori-fy our Maker Made to love God Made to love each oth-er

Made to love our-self Made to glo-ri-fy our cre-a-
Made to love our-self Made to glo-ri-fy our cre-a-

THANK YOU

Walter Van Der Haas
Peter-Paul Van Lelyveld

258

Martin G. Schneider

1. Thank You   for giv - ing   me   the   morn - ing,   Thank You   for ev - 'ry   day that's
2. Thank You   for all   my   friends and broth - ers,   Thank You   for all   the   men that
3. Thank You   I   have my   oc - cu - pa - tion,   Thank You   for ev - 'ry   pleas - ure

new,   Thank You   that I   can know my   wor - ries   Can   be   cast on   You. __
live,   Thank You   for e - ven   great - est   en - e - mies   I   can for - give. __
small,   Thank You   for mu - sic,   light and   glad - ness,   Thank You for them   all. ____

* After stanza three, the key of each succeeding stanza may rise one-half step, if so desired.

4. Thank You for many little sorrows,
Thank You for ev'ry kindly word,
Thank You that ev'rywhere Your guidance
Reaches ev'rywhere

5. Thank You _ I see Your Word has meaning,
Thank You _ I know Your Spirit here,
Thank You because You love all People,
Those both far and near.

6. Thank You, O Lord _ You spoke unto us,
Thank You, that for our words you care,
Thank You, O Lord _ You came among us,
Bread and wine to share.

7. Thank You, O Lord _ Your love is boundless,
Thank You that I am full of You,
Thank You, _ You make me feel so glad
And thankful as I do.

259 SING UNTO GOD

Psalm 68:4

Sing un-to God, sing praises to His name. Sing un-to God, sing praise to His name. Ex-tol Him that rideth on the heavens by His name, ex-tol Him that rideth on the heavens by His name, Ex-tol Him that rideth on the heavens by His name, by His name, JAH. And re-joice be-fore Him and re-joice be-fore Him, and re-joice, re-joice be-

fore   Him   And re -   fore _____   Him!

THE BOND OF LOVE   **260**

John 17:23; Eph. 4:1-3; Col. 2:2

Words and Music by
Otis Skillings

1. We   are   one   in   the   bond   of   love;   We   are
2. Let   us   sing   now, ___ ev - 'ry,   one;   Let   us

one   in   the bond   of   love. ____ We have joined   our   spir - it with the
feel   His ___ love   be - gun. ____ Let   us   join   our   hands, __ that the

Spir - it   of   God;   We   are   one   in   the   bond   of   love.
world   will __ know   We   are   one   in   the   bond   of   love.

261   IN THE GARDEN

Words and Music by
C. Austin Miles

1. I come to the gar-den a-lone ___ While the dew is still on the
2. He speaks, and the sound of His voice ___ Is so sweet the birds hush their
3. I'd stay in the gar-den with Him ___ Though the night a-round me be

ros-es; And the voice I hear fall-ing on my ear The Son of God dis-
sing-ing; And the me-lo-dy that He gave to me With-in my heart is
fall-ing; But He bids me go thru the voice of woe, His voice to me is

clos - es.
ring - ing. And He walks with me and He talks with me, And He
call - ing.

Chorus

tells me I am His own. ___ And the joy we share as we

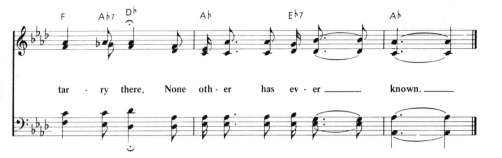

tar - ry there, None oth - er has ev - er _____ known. _____

O COME, LET US ADORE HIM 262

Adapted

From Canrus Diversi

1. O come, let us a - dore _ Him; O come, let us a - dore Him;
2. For He a - lone is wor - thy; For He a - lone is _ wor - thy;
3. For Je - sus is our Sav - ior; For Je - sus is our _ Sav - ior;
4. And Je - sus is our broth - er; And Je - sus is our _ broth - er;
5. We kneel in ad - o - ra - tion; We kneel in ad - o - ra - tion;
6. O praise Him, al - le - lu - ia! O praise Him, al - le - lu - ia!

O come, let us a - dore Him, _ Christ _____ the Lord.
For He _ a - lone is wor - thy, _ Christ _____ the Lord.
For Je - sus is our Sav - ior, _ Christ _____ the Lord.
And Je - sus is our broth - er, _ Christ _____ the Lord.
We kneel _ in ad - o - ra - tion. _ Christ _____ the Lord.
O praise Him, al - le - lu - ia! _ Christ _____ the Lord.

263 NOW THANK WE ALL OUR GOD

Martin Rinkart
Tr. Catherine Winkworth

Johann Cruger

1. Now thank we all our God, With heart and hands and voic - es,
2. O may this boun - teous God, Through all our life be near us,
3. All praise and thanks to God, The Fa - ther now be giv - en,

Who won - drous things has done, In whom His world re - joic - es;
With ev - er joy - ful hearts, And bless - ed peace to cheer us;
The Son and Him who reigns With them in high - est heav - en;

Who from our moth - er's arms Has blessed us on our way
And keep us in His grace, And guide us when per - plexed,
The one e - ter - nal God, Whom earth and heaven a - dore;

With count - less gifts of love, And still is ours to - day.
And free us from all ills, In this world and the next.
For thus it was, is now, And shall be ev - er - more!

DOXOLOGY

264

Thomas Ken

Jimmy Owens

Praise God ___ from ___ whom all bless - ings

flow. Praise Him, ___ all crea - tures here ___ be -

low. Praise Him ___ a - bove, ye heav - en - ly

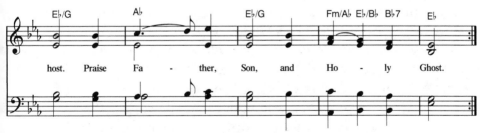

host. Praise Fa - ther, Son, and Ho - ly Ghost.

Prelude
Opening Hymn
The Welcome
Announcements
Congregational Hymn

CONFESSION

Lord, we need Your mercy. In this hour, help us to see our sin and pain and pray for a fresh start. Help us to see the shortcomings in our lives and look to You for the answers to our problems. Give us a new vision of what life can be like. Teach us to hope, to love, to give and to have faith. Lord, we need Your mercy.

ABSOLUTION - THE GOOD NEWS

Our God has heard the cries and felt your pain and has had mercy on us. God has seen our need and provided for our salvation; seen our condition and provided the solution; seen our heart and given us a Savior. Through the death and resurrection of Jesus Christ, our sin is no longer the weight that holds us down. We are free to live in victory, free from the sin of our self deceit and free from Satan's power. Praise God for goodness.

AFFIRMATION OF FAITH

We believe in God, the Creator of all things, the source of all goodness and love...We believe in Jesus Christ, the Son of God, true God yet true man. He was crucified, died and was buried for our sin that we might be free and know the joy of life. He was raised on the third day and ascended to heaven, and will come again in power and glory to judge both the living and the dead...We believe in the Holy Spirit, the power of God at work inside of us...We believe in the church of God, the people of faith throughout the world...We believe that our sin is forgiven and that we will live together with God for now and throughout eternity. Amen.

THE MESSAGE FROM THE WORD
Offering
SPECIAL MUSIC
A time for prayer (you are invited to come to the altar to pray)
Benediction
Closing Hymn
Postlude   © 1992 Handt Hanson

Prelude
Opening Hymn
Opening Prayer
Welcome to Worship
Distribution of Welcome Folders
Announcements
A Hymn of Faith

CONFESSION

Lord, we confess our lack of faith. We see a glimpse of what we ought to be and we know we fall short of the goal. We desire faith that is solid and unchanging, yet we crumble under trials and temptations. We want to be strong, but we know our own weakness. Our sinful condition strips us of any spiritual gain that we humanly devise. Lord, forgive us. Accept us as we are, unworthy for the task, yet gifted for Your purposes. Give us Your gift of faith.

ABSOLUTION

Our God is a great God and knows our needs for all areas of our life. God knows our weakness and our unbelieving hearts, yet loves us enough to die on a cross and provide forgiveness of our sin. Now the focus is not on the faith that we can muster, but on the great gifts that our Lord gives daily as we live in trust. God has given us the gift of faith, faith for the moment, faith for every trial, faith for every temptation, faith for every difficult situation. Praise God for this inexpressible gift of faith.
Hymn of Praise
Scripture lessons for the Day

AFFIRMATION OF FAITH

I have faith in God, in response to overwhelming love...I believe that God created me and all that I have, and has given to me gifts beyond measure...I have faith in Jesus, who emptied Himself out of His love for me...I believe that Christ died on a cross for my sin, conquered death and the power of evil, and was raised to life on the third day. His death is mine, His resurrection is mine, new life is mine because of Jesus' words and work...I believe in the Holy Spirit in response to overwhelming love...I believe that the Holy Spirit is present here among us and lives within each person. The Spirit continues to call people by the Gospel, and creates and builds the church of Christ. Through the power of the Spirit I have power to stand in strength and against all adversity...I believe that Jesus is preparing a place for me and will come again to take each of us to be with Him. Amen.
Offering
Special Music
Sermon
Prayers (you are invited to the altar to pray)
Benediction
Closing Hymn
Postlude

Prelude   (Communion)
Opening Hymn
Opening Prayer
Welcome to Worship
Distribution of Welcome Pads
Announcements
Hymn
WE CONFESS OUR SIN (together)
Lord, we confess our sin, You have promised to provide for all
of our needs, and yet we mistrust Your promise. We know the
futility of our own ambitions and our inability to do that which
we desire. Today we need to recognize the sin within us, and ask
that you would forgive us. Lord, in Your mercy, give us daily
bread, not only for our bodies, but as food for our spirits.
Forgive our sin and cleanse us so that we can be pleasing in Your
sight and ministers in Your service.
WE HEAR THE GOOD NEWS
Our God is a great God, providing for all our needs, giving us
daily bread and supplies for every spiritual need. Our sin no
longer controls us. Our response to God's love is the focus for
our lives. The death of Jesus Christ has paid the cost of our sin
and has set us free to live in victory. We are forgiven. We are
daughters and sons of God. We are ministers to each other.
Praise God for the daily provision for our every need.
AFFIRMATION OF FAITH
I believe in God, who has created all things and continues to
create new life within us...I believe in Jesus, son of God, son of
man, the Savior of the world. By His life, His death and
resurrection, I can know the true depth of human possibility, and
experience the true joy of an abundant life....I believe that the
Holy Spirit is present, now and always, calling us to faith, giving
us gifts and empowering us for service...I believe that the
community of believers called the church can experience the
fullness of life through the word, the sacraments, and all that we
do.
Sermon
Offering (all the gifts, including the elements, are brought to
the altar)
Special Music
COMMUNION LITURGY
The Invitation
Leader: Welcome to the celebration! God who supplies our
             every need has given us this meal to share.
People: Lord, we thank You for the bread of eternal life.
Leader: We come to the table, acknowledging our
             shortcomings and our need to experience Your
             presence in bread and wine.
People: Lord, we thank You for the bread of eternal life.

The Words of Institution For the Bread - Matthew 26:26,27
The Words of Institution For the Wine - Matthew 26: 28,29
The Lord's Prayer
The Distribution
Distribution Hymns (sung together during the distribution)
The Blessing
The Benediction
Closing Hymn
Postlude
                                    © 1992 Handt Hanson

Prelude
Opening Hymn
Opening Prayer
Welcome to Worship
Distribution of Welcome Folders
Congregational Hymn

CONFESSION

Lord, God of our tomorrows, we confess our sinful condition before You. We desire something better than what we have and what we are. We know ourselves too well and see our human frailty. We know that our temporary gods are vulnerable and will crumble under the test. We realize that our desires are fickle and backfire on us at the worst times. God of our tomorrows, give us Your forgiveness. Let us see today the promise of something better in our lives.

ABSOLUTION

Our God is a tomorrow God, who knows our past and knows where we are headed. We trust a God who knows our needs and desires each of us come daily in prayer. As we confess our sins, God is faithful and will forgive our sin and make us clean from all unrighteousness. God always promises us something better, because of the miracle of forgiveness and love. Praise God from whom all blessings flow.

Hymn of Praise
Scripture Lesson for the Day

AFFIRMATION OF FAITH
      Apostles Creed
Offering
Special Music
Sermon
Prayers (you are invited to the altar to pray)
Hymn for Prayer
Benediction

Leader:	Go in peace. You are the forgiven people of God.
People:	We will celebrate forgiveness in every tomorrow. We will celebrate forgiveness in the week ahead through acts of kindness, times of listening concern, and deeds of generosity.
Leader:	Go in peace. You are the forgiven people of God.
People:	We have heard the Good News. We will share the Good News.
Leader:	The Lord be with you. Go and serve in Jesus' name. Amen.

Closing Hymn
Postlude

© 1992 Handt Hanson

Prelude
Opening Hymn
Opening Prayer
Welcome to Worship
Distribution of Welcome Pads
Announcements
Hymn
CONFESSION
Lord, we come before You in prayer today, asking for forgiveness. We have not loved as we ought to love, we have not given as we ought to give, and we have fallen short of the mark of truly being Your obedient sons and daughters. We recognize our sin and in this moment of silence, we privately remember our shortcomings in love and life. *(Silence for reflection.)*
FORGIVENESS
God, our heavenly Creator, hears the prayers of all people and answers those prayers. Our prayer for forgiveness is answered in the person of Jesus Christ, God's Son, who died for our sin that we might have new life. The distance between God and ourselves has been brought together by love made perfect in the sacrifice of Jesus. To those who believe God's word of truth comes power to be the people of God. Praise God for the gift of love to us.
Hymn of Praise
Scripture Readings for the Day
Affirmation of Faith - The Nicene Creed
Pastoral Prayers
Sermon
Offering (the elements and the tithes and offerings are brought to the altar)
Special Music
THE COMMUNION

Leader:	We declare ourselves to be Easter people.
People:	We have come to share in the table that He has prepared for us.
Leader	He took the bad news of sin and guilt and changed it to good news through His dying and rising for us.
People:	We are here to celebrate that Good News and the presence of Christ with us.
Leader:	And He took the bread, blessed it and broke it. He said to His disciples-
People:	"Take, eat; this is my body."
Leader:	Also, He took a cup of wine. After saying thanks, He gave it to them saying-
People:	"Drink of it, all of you, for this is my blood of the covenant. It is poured out for the forgiveness of sins. Do this to remember me."
Leader:	We thank You, Lord God, for these elements given in love for us. Accept us, forgive us, and heal us - that we might live lives that are pleasing to you.

The Lord's Prayer
The Distribution
Distribution Hymns (sung by the Cong. during the distribution)
The Blessing
The Benediction
Closing Hymn
Postlude

TOPICAL INDEX

Compiled by Rev. Mark T. Hannemann, Dale Pust, and Dave Anderson

SCRIPTURAL INDEX

compiled by Rev. Mark T. Hannemann

INDEX

*Indicates page number in first edition.

*Indicates page number in first edition.